THE
SHIVFIT
WAY

THE SHIVFIT WAY

A COMPREHENSIVE
FUNCTIONAL FITNESS PROGRAMME

SHIVOHAM

WITH
SHRENIK AVLANI

EBURY
PRESS

An imprint of Penguin Random House

EBURY PRESS

USA | Canada | UK | Ireland | Australia
New Zealand | India | South Africa | China

Ebury Press is part of the Penguin Random House group of companies
whose addresses can be found at global.penguinrandomhouse.com

Published by Penguin Random House India Pvt. Ltd
4th Floor, Capital Tower 1, MG Road,
Gurugram 122 002, Haryana, India

Penguin
Random House
India

First published in Ebury Press by Penguin Random House India 2017

ISBN 9788184004359

Typeset in Sabon by Manipal Digital Systems, Manipal
Printed at Repro India Limited

www.penguin.co.in

MIX
Paper from
responsible sources
FSC® C047271

I dedicate this book to my satguru,
Yogiraj Siddhanath Gurunath, without
whom nothing would have been possible

Contents

Contents

Introduction

Start. Don't think. Don't plan. Don't wait for the 'right time'. Start.

Go on, get up and do ten push-ups, fifteen squats, twenty jumping jacks. Right now.

Now that you have started, it's going to be easier for you to motivate yourself to spare a little time from your busy schedule for your physical and mental well-being.

Starting is the biggest challenge.

I meet several people at my CrossFit boxes[1] in Mumbai, and during my fitness awareness tours across the country, who are extremely motivated and driven and want to embrace a healthy lifestyle

---

[1] They are called boxes because CrossFit gyms are nearly bare without any machines like a regular gym. They have only basic equipment such as weights, kettlebells and Roman rings.

that incorporates exercise in their daily routine. But they haven't been able to do so as they keep telling themselves, 'I will start working out tomorrow', or 'I am going to start exercising today . . . after office in the evening' but remain stuck at the starting line. In today's competitive and hyper-social world, there are various pressures, plenty of commitments and endless distractions. Whatever little time you get, you probably want to put your feet up, let your hair down and escape the constant demands of your hectic twenty-first century life.

I believe getting people to start exercising is the first, most important, and also the most difficult task. Once past this stage, things are simpler. Most people, more often than not, come back after the first week of working out with us. So begin *today*. It might feel like a punishment initially, but keep at it for a week before deciding if you really want to give up.

How did I get over my own starting hiccups?

I might have had the same trouble as most people do but for my dad. Given the way I put off returning calls, sending emails and doing my paperwork, had it not been for my father I might have found it very difficult to start exercising. In my mind I have it down to the minute as to when I will return that phone call, click *send* on that long-pending email and get my paperwork in order—just like most people tell me when and how they plan to start working out the next day, or once the weekend parties are through. But when it comes to exercise and sports, I don't procrastinate, I don't think, I don't plan. Thanks to dad (and borrowing one of the most popular marketing lines by a sportswear company), I just do it.

When I was five months old, my dad decided he had seen his fill of me flapping my arms and legs around on the bed. As cute as my mother may have thought that was, my father had had enough. He took me to the swimming pool at Khar Gymkhana Club in Mumbai. In those five months, he had noticed that I was very fond of water. He decided swimming, if anything at all, was my future. He took me into the pool. Since five-month-olds do not have very developed memories, I don't remember any of this. But my parents have narrated the story so many times—with pride, I must add—to me, my brother, uncles and aunts, friends, relatives and whosoever was a willing audience, that I have it down to the last syllable.

My dad would take my brother and me to the pool every Sunday without fail. We would flap our hands and legs and try to stay afloat every time he would slip his hands out from under us. When I think about it now, we must have swallowed a lot of water back then—this explains how I learnt to keep myself hydrated at all times! This is, in fact, another life lesson my dad taught me quite early. It was a rather unusual way of doing it, but one that was effective all the same.

Once we were old enough and did not need constant attention and supervision, the two of us would race each other, compete to see who could stay underwater longer or dive further, while dad would do his own thing, sneaking in a look once in a while to see what his sons were up to. Every time he saw us race, his face would break out in a smile. That's how my fitness journey began at the infantile age of five months. Instead of a bottle of milk and play gym, I was holding floating tubes and splashing around in a pool. That's one reason why, when it came to sports or exercise, I have not once had any starting trouble. At the age of five, I started swimming competitively and went on to participate in national-level events before my eleventh birthday. At fifteen years, my uncle gave me his old dumb-bells and I started lifting weights. In college, I captained the water polo team and then moved to Australia to study animation. A year into the course, I dropped out of college to become a fitness trainer. My mother wasn't very happy with this decision, more so because she had spent a lot of money to send me abroad to study and make a career. But I was simply following the path my father, without knowing its repercussions, had put me on very early in life.

At my gym and with friends, I do what my dad did for me early in my life—help people start. If it means being strict, I will be the meanest drill master they have ever met. If they need to be coaxed, I will patiently talk to them till they are ready. If the motivation to start is missing, they will find more than enough of it from each and every member who trains in my CrossFit boxes. Once you start, there is no looking back. The biggest hurdle has been crossed.

This book is also meant to help the busy, working, studying, socializing, career-oriented men and women turn away from their iPads and smartphones and take a look at their bodies and what they need.

Remember growing up as a kid in the 1980s' and 1990s' India? There were no iPads, iPhones, cable TV and PlayStation Portables. For us, the Mumbai kids, time off from studies meant running amok in the streets with other children from the neighbourhood, cycling around Bandra in gangs, playing *Chor Police*, cricket and the Indian, more aggressive version of *I Spy* called *Dabba I Spy*, and football, thrown in with some occasional fighting. For those who grew up at a time when sweating over transferring contacts from a micro SIM card to its nano version wasn't all time-consuming, when upgrading to iPad's retina display was not the biggest decision of the week, you need to get back to those proverbial good old days and find inspiration in the fact that you didn't have any of the medical problems and conditions that plague you now. The worst that you had to deal with back then was a nasty bruise from a fall down the stairs or being hit by a cricket ball. Go back to being a child once again. You will be much happier. Getting back to an active life will help you beat, and keep in check, the weight issues, hypertension, blood pressure, thyroid problems, cholesterol levels and heart problems that your routine medical check-up hurls at you twice a year.

For me, working out has been as much of an engrossing and rigorous physical journey as it has been a spiritual one. All of us have heard about runners who feel that running is a meditative experience. I feel something similar when I am sweating it out in the box with the barbells and kettlebells, doing pull-ups, squats, dead lifts, burpees and push-ups. Personally, I evolved a lot as my own fitness journey progressed—today I am more calm and self-conscious. I am more aware of what my mind, body and soul need, unlike the angry, petulant young teenager I used to be. Getting to know my inner self has not only helped me perform better in other walks of life but also made me physically stronger and my mind clearer. Weighing in at sixty-five kg and squatting with 140 kg cannot be explained in any other way. Yoga and meditation have played a big role. I have seen several friends, who took to working out regularly, become improved versions of themselves. I shall talk about this aspect of working out in a later chapter.

This book also serves as a ready reckoner for those looking for a quick workout no matter where they are—in terms of location, ability and fitness levels. There are not only illustrations and pictorial representations of all exercises, stretches and asanas mentioned here but also a guide for planning your workout each day, which can be done by anyone, irrespective of age, sex, strength and stamina. First of all, familiarize yourself with the correct form of each exercise. If you have trouble understanding the pictures and instructions in the book, please double-check on my YouTube channel: Shivoham Shivfit. I have listed a number of reliable Internet sources that can help you achieve the correct form.

Nutrition: the thing most people overlook when talking about health and fitness is also decoded and explained here. There is a popular saying, and schools of fitness concur, that fitness is 30 per cent exercise and 70 per cent what you eat. If you want to start by changing your eating habits, turn to Chapter 5. Here you will find information about foods that are good for you and those that you must absolutely avoid. It also helps you decide, based on your body type, how often you can cheat and give in to that chocolate craving or the urge to have the tangy chaat during your trip to New Delhi. I have based my recommendations, firstly, on sound scientific data and studies and, secondly, on what has worked for me and those I have trained over the years. I have seen the results of what a good diet can achieve. Frankly, with proper food, you can work wonders with surprisingly little amounts of exercise.

This book has been meticulously planned keeping in mind the needs of busy people on the go. I have also taken into consideration that my readers are likely to be those who are new to exercise as well as those who are on advanced levels of training. The workout directory in this book has been designed with immense care so that both newbies and advanced athletes benefit from it and can use it with ease.

At the bottom of every tenth page are workouts that you need to do on the day you reach that page. Workouts towards the beginning of the book are easy as they are meant for beginners. The difficulty level increases as you move on. If you are to stay true to the routine outlined here and your progress is as expected, then you should be challenged just a wee bit more by each successive workout without feeling overwhelmed by what stares you in the

face. The workouts are meant to focus on your
entire body and on the large muscle groups (thighs,
hamstrings, back and shoulders) that need to be
strong to effectively carry out day-to-day tasks. The
smaller muscles, such as biceps and triceps, or what
people call arms, require no special attention. They
are engaged and develop on their own as a result of
the complex movements that exercises like squats,
dead lifts, push-press, pull-ups and push-ups entail.
No, you don't need to spend hours doing bicep
curls and tricep pull-downs for those chiselled arms.
The routines recommended in my workouts are a
mix of weightlifting, dynamic explosive training,
body weight exercises, gymnastics and cardiovascular exercises. Some routines do require some
basic equipment, such as kettlebells, dumb-bells
and barbells. If you have them, or have access to
them, great. If not, use substitutes like water bottles,
watermelons, and buckets filled with sand, water
and stones. You can easily replace dumb-bells with
one or two-litre plastic bottles that you are usually
left with after a party at home. Just fill two of them
with the same amount of water and use them. Yes,
it will feel different, but it will help you improve
balance and make your grip stronger. If you want to
make them heavier, fill the bottles with sand. In case
you need heavier weights, which you should slowly
build up to, use buckets. Fill up a bucket with sand

or water. If you are using water, make sure you don't fill it beyond the halfway mark, or else it will spill at the slightest movement. You could use this for dead lifts and goblet squats, which have been explained in the exercise glossary.

There, you have no more excuses. Let's begin.

1

Fitness

The Shoddy Way

I was young. I had flat, hard abs. I could lift more than my body weight in the gym. People in Australia even hired me for personal training at their elite, air-conditioned gyms. I was fit. Or at least I thought I was.

Then I went for my first CrossFit session. It was a simple pull-up, push-up, squat routine—five pull-ups, ten push-ups and fifteen squats back-to-back for five minutes. 'Five minutes only?' an overconfident voice sniggered in my head. I went at it with all the speed I could muster and with a smile plastered on my face. After two minutes, a wide open mouth gasping for air had dislodged the smile. Another minute later, chest and head hanging over the legs and both palms pressed against the knees were just about keeping me from tumbling over. By the fourth minute, the insides of my stomach were churning. By the end of

3

the fifth minute, I was flat on my back, lying spread-eagled in a pool of sweat and drool. No sooner had I felt some air reach my lungs, than my intestines pushed everything out with such great force that I bounced like a spring and puked right there. The remains of a banana and pre-workout shake made for a perfect example of projectile motion that we studied in school. Needless to say, it formed an ugly, smelly puddle on the gym floor. I didn't even have time to go out and save myself some embarrassment. So much for being fit.

I had moved to Melbourne in 2004 to get a degree in animation. All right, there was a girl involved. There always is if a young man of twenty years goes ahead and does something as drastic as that.

I had met Natalie in Mumbai in 2003. She had come down to the city for a trip, and we met on one wild night of clubbing through common friends. We connected immediately; there was a spark between us. With every passing day, the spark grew stronger and many things were singed. Eventually, her holiday ended and she flew back to Melbourne. A month after she left, a shoot for a film took me to Sydney. My stars had aligned perfectly, or I got lucky, depending on how you look at it.

My work in Sydney was for just ten days and I was supposed to fly back to Mumbai after that. But I headed to Melbourne instead to celebrate my birthday with Natalie and ended up staying there for three months. It was bliss. I returned to India when my bank account indicated that I was nearing a state college kids readily identify with—being broke. I tried getting into the merchant navy but couldn't make the cut, though not because of my fitness. I brainstormed and finally decided that I wanted to study animation to make a career in films or advertising. My parents were happy with the idea since my dad was in the photography business and had done rather well for himself. And then I timidly dropped the bomb—it would be in Melbourne. My mother was livid, but you know Indian parents. They love indulging in their kids, especially when it comes to education. She gave in, paid my fees and booked me a ticket. I packed my bags for Melbourne yet again in 2004, thinking of Natalie starry-eyed. The joys of youth.

The first thing I did in Melbourne after joining college was to enrol in a gym. Later, I got a part-time job at the same gym—a leading global chain which has a presence in India—selling memberships and attending to the front desk. We lived opposite a beach in Melbourne. Day in and day out, we could see people surfing, kitesurfing, skateboarding, playing volleyball, running and working out on the beach with their sun-tanned, chiselled bodies. With a laptop, a bottle of Coke and a packet of chips on my desk, I would stare at length at the people outdoors sweating it out, having fun and living life.

I was at my desk by the window one pleasant day, working on a college project and getting more and more frustrated at the sight of each surfer and skateboarder. The project was especially boring and I couldn't concentrate on anything but the people outside. That's when I had a 'get-a-life' moment. I went to the gym and asked the manager if I could get a full-time job as a personal trainer. He had seen me work out. I was in decent shape and had abs, so that clinched the deal. I called up my mother.

The conversation went something like this: *Hello. Hello. Mummy, I don't care about animation, that's not my calling. Beta . . . I can't do it any more.* Sobbing sounds. *Mom, please calm down, I will figure something out.* Sniff, sniff, sniff. *I have already got a job as a personal trainer.* The yelling began. *Mom, I love you. Bye.* The yelling continued. I hung up.

Life was sweet till I went for my first CrossFit session.

I was perplexed, angry and embarrassed. As a personal trainer at a global gym chain, I was used to people complimenting me on my body and fitness level. I had seen and heard many clients complain about feeling nauseous after a short session on the treadmill or bench-pressing. I would tell them that the feeling was normal for someone who hadn't experienced any physical exertion in a long time. 'The fitter you get, the less dizzy you feel after a workout,' was how I explained the situation to them. And now here I was, puking my guts out after just five minutes of simple body weight exercises.

At first, doubts started creeping into my head—doubts about my fitness. After the initial panic, as I thought more and more about what had happened during my first CrossFit session, I started asking questions: What is fitness?

It is a simple question. But how exactly do you define fitness? What are the parameters to measure it? Is there any scale on which you can measure a person's fitness levels? Are strength and fitness connected? If there is a link, what is it?

Whatever answers I had to these questions before my disappointing CrossFit session were not valid any more. I needed new and more accurate answers. A fresh start and a new approach offered some clarity. To this day, as science progresses and research in health and fitness gets more funding, technology and support, the answers keep evolving.

So, what exactly is fitness?

The Merriam-Webster dictionary defines fitness as 'the quality or state of being fit', while fit is defined as 'sound physically and mentally'. Though the word was first used in 1580 AD, its dictionary definition does not tell us much about what fitness actually is.

We have seen triathletes compete in Ironman races, which involve swimming 3.86 kilometres, followed by cycling 180.25 km and then immediately running a full marathon of 42.195 km, being crowned the fittest men and women in the world. But put them in a gym and ask them to lift weights, and you will find that they fare rather poorly. Even a boy or girl of average strength will be able to lift more than the fittest men and women on earth if endurance sport is the measure of fitness, as it mainly enhances the aerobic capacity of an individual.

But walk into a weightlifting clinic or lifters training for the Olympics and you would find the smallest of them lifting much more than their body weight. Lifters usually describe their colleagues as strong, not fit. Now ask them to run a couple of kilometres or swim just 500 metres. You are most likely to see them struggling and gasping for breath pretty quickly. So, strength alone also cannot be a parameter to measure fitness.

Clearly, fitness means different things to different people. Depending on who you ask, fitness is likely to be defined in terms of things people are good at or specialize in. For a runner, being able to run a full marathon in under four hours is being fit. For a body-builder, big muscles are clear indicators of fitness. Then again, talk to weightlifters, and they will tell you that their ability to lift weights three times heavier than themselves is proof of their fitness. For the average person, fitness could mean something as simple as going through an entire day of work and having enough energy to indulge in their hobbies or run and play freely with their kids without feeling exhausted.

In the many years I have spent in this industry, and during the course of my own journey, I have come to realize that no single parameter can measure fitness. Several factors measure different attributes of your body, and the ones you pay more attention to depend on which school of fitness you follow. For example, if you believe having sculpted abs is a mark of fitness, then you will strive for low body fat percentage. For others, it could be achieving the ideal weight according to their height and body type.

Since I believe in and practise CrossFit, I follow its founder Greg Glassman's definition of fitness, which is based on the following ten general physical skills:

Cardiovascular or respiratory endurance: The ability of the body to gather, process and deliver oxygen to its different parts.

Stamina: The ability of the body systems to process, deliver, store and utilize energy.

Strength: The ability of a muscular unit, or combination of muscular units, to apply force.

Flexibility: The ability to maximize range of motion at a given joint.

Power: The ability of a muscular unit, or combination of muscular units, to apply maximum force in minimum time.

Speed: The ability to minimize the time cycle of a repeated movement.

Coordination: The ability to combine several distinct movement patterns into a singular distinct movement.

Agility: The ability to minimize transition time from one movement pattern to another.

Balance: The ability to control the placement of the body's centre of gravity with regard to its support base.

Workout No. 1

Five pull-ups, ten push-ups, fifteen squats for five minutes, non-stop.

This is the simplest, yet one of the toughest, exercise routines to pull off. Since it's your first time working out with my routine, your aim here should be to last for a full five minutes. Pace yourself accordingly. Don't worry about the numbers. A word of warning: Do not start out too fast no matter how fit you are.

Accuracy: The ability to control a movement in a given direction or at a given intensity.[1]

The US Marines, who are considered to be among the fittest people in the world, felt the need to change their training methods in 2006 after interviewing veterans who had served in Iraq and Afghanistan. The paper titled, 'A Concept for Functional Fitness',[2] acknowledges that aerobic training should not be the primary physical goal of the modern US Marines, but rather core strength, endurance, speed, and coordination. Approved by Lieutenant General James Amos, deputy commandant for Combat Development and Integration, Marine Corps Combat Development Command, in 2006, it points out that the Marines need to follow a training regimen followed by professional athletes.

Some of the major points addressed in the paper were:

– A balanced approach must be used to develop power, strength, flexibility, speed, endurance, agility and coordination.

– A programme should have intensity and great variety.

---

[1] Greg Glassman, *What is Fitness* (*The CrossFit Journal*, 2002), https://journal.crossfit.com/article/what-is-fitness

[2] United States Marine Corps, 'A Concept For Functional Fitness' (2006), http://library.crossfit.com/free/pdf/USMCFunctionalFitnessConcept.pdf

– A programme is characteristically general and well-balanced. The intensity leads to positive physical adaptation and the variety keeps the stimulus fresh yet helps avoid over-training related injuries.

The paper also stressed the fact that the Marines needed a comprehensive fitness programme that developed core strength, endurance, speed, and coordination.

Just like the Marines and Glassman, I belong to the school of thought that treats fitness as all-inclusive and measures it in terms of multiple skills and parameters. If you can lift a lot of weight but cannot run even a kilometre without trouble, to me you are not fit. If you can run a lot but cannot even lift twenty per cent of your body weight, you again belong to the cadre of the unfit according to me. In the competitive twenty-first century that we live in, specialization in just one area of fitness doesn't work. It worked in the days of Arnold Schwarzenegger when bodybuilding was big. But today, in order to survive the challenges life throws at you—be it in terms of the long working hours or the physical toll day-to-day life and pollution take on our bodies— you need to be fit like Rocky, the one played by Sylvester Stallone in the timeless Oscar-winning film by the same name. Like Rocky, you not only need to be strong and powerful but must also have the ability to move quickly and lightly, besides having enough endurance and stamina to stay on your feet for long hours.

The brand of fitness that I promote and practise will hold you in good stead in all walks of life, make you better and more efficient at daily tasks, and leave you with much more energy and strength even after an exceptionally stressful day.

All the exercises that we do in my gyms don't need fancy machines or equipment—no cables, multi-gyms or ab-crunchers that you see in the others. We only use barbells, weights, dumb-bells, kettlebells and the pull-up bar. On many days, we only do body weight exercises, which mean we do not even use the equipment listed above. Most of the exercises involve movements that we use in day-to-day life, such as lifting things from the ground (dead lift), sitting down and getting back up (squats), climbing (step-ups), pulling (high-pulls, pull-ups) and pushing (push-ups, shoulder press), which is why CrossFit is also known as a functional fitness regimen. All of these exercises are complex movements and engage your big muscle groups, such as legs, back, buttocks and chest, besides activating the core.

So, where do we start with you? With the basics. No weights till the time you get your basic movements correct. Your mantra for this phase should be 'keep it simple'. It is important that you pay close attention to form and do not compromise on it at all. Poor form is like a bad habit—very easy to pick up but very difficult to get rid of. If you are not sure and are confused despite the illustrations in this book, please turn to the instructional videos on my YouTube channel—Shivoham Shivfit—or any other, or on any good Olympic weightlifting site such as www.catalystathletics.com, or the official CrossFit website. See those videos and check your form, or ask someone to help you with it. You can also take videos of yourself doing the exercises and then compare those with the ones on the instructional channels. Get your form correct: it's the only way to avoid injuries and ensure the best results in the smallest time frame.

Now, here are the exercises that will put you on the road to complete fitness:

Squats: Have you ever noticed how effortlessly toddlers can go down into a sitting position and then get back up with equally remarkable ease, without twitching in discomfort or throwing their arms around to find some balance? If not, observe them closely. Their spine is straight, the knees are in line with the ankles and pointing outwards and the weight is on their heels and butt. These little kids do not have muscles or bones as strong as yours. Whenever they walk, their parents and caretakers keep an eye on them, partly out of the joy of seeing them learn to walk and also to ensure that they do not have a bad fall because their sense of balance is still developing. But watch them squat and there are no such worries. As a fitness coach, I absolutely love seeing how perfectly they squat. Their form is immaculate and the effort is minimal. They also squat much more in a day than their parents will in a whole week, even if they go to a gym.

Though extremely simple and basic—anyone who has ever used an Indian-style loo will shout out in chorus—a squat is one of the toughest exercises. This is the first movement I teach people.

Start from the standing position, feet shoulder width apart, arms hanging by your side and your gaze fixed straight ahead. Now, as you gradually raise your hands up to shoulder level, push your butt back and start sitting down till it goes below your knees. Make sure that you don't push your knees forward. Quickly look down and check if you can see your toes. If you can, you are doing fine as far as form is concerned. If you see your knees and no toes, then you are doing it wrong. You need to consciously make an effort to keep your knees from slipping forward and push them outwards slightly to the side. If your form is correct, try to go all the way to the position you would be in while sitting over an Indian-style loo. Of the two ranges of motion mentioned above, hold your position for three seconds on whatever range you reach. Now, pushing your heels down, push your hips up and return to the starting position. Repeat this till you get your form right and achieve the full range of motion.

Once you have mastered this exercise, you can skip the step where you hold your squat for three seconds and start doing quick squats in one smooth motion.

There are some basic things you must remember in order to ensure squats prove to be useful and a tad easier: push your knees outwards if keeping your feet parallel makes you lose balance or shift weight forward, and let your toes point outwards slightly. Finally, raise your arms up to shoulder level while you descend and bring them down as you ascend to improve balance.

Stuart Phillips, a PhD holder, a professor of kinesiology at McMaster University in Canada and an expert on the effects of resistance training on the human body, says squats are the best exercise. In an interview,[3] he said the squat 'activates the body's biggest muscles, those in the buttocks, back and legs'. He recommends twenty-five squats at a time to be a very potent exercise and asks people to start using a barbell once free or body weight squats become easy.

Squats are one of the best exercises for the lower body. One reason is that it is a multi-joint exercise that targets all the muscles in the hips, glutes (muscles in the buttock) and thighs. This means you will

---

[3] Gretchen Reynolds, 'What's The Single Best Exercise', *The New York Times Magazine*, April 15 2011, http://www.nytimes.com/2011/04/17/magazine/mag-17exercise-t.html

end up having better, toned and tighter buttocks, hamstrings, thighs and hips. It also activates the core (abdomen and lower back muscles), which means that you are working your abs at the same time.

Millions of people in our cities, villages and all over the world sit down in a squat position to rest. So stick to doing full squats. Half squats do not work all the muscles, especially the quadricep (the large fleshy part in the front of the thigh that extends down from the top of the leg till your knees), and do not engage the core as much as full squats do. Moreover, half squats overwork the hamstring (the muscle at the back of the thigh that runs from below your buttocks till the back of the knees), which can lead to problems like stiff glutes, hips and lower back.

As great an exercise that it is, squats have a lot of stigma attached to them. It is mainly hearsay and rumours; started probably by those who were injured because of poor form or trying to lift much more than they were physically capable of. Either way, the whiff-whaff about squats being bad for the knees, bad for the back and other such jibber-jabber is just that. Scientific and physiological research has carried out extensive studies with athletes and novices the world over and found absolutely nothing wrong with it. On the contrary, all findings have listed a whole lot of positive effects of squatting as an exercise. In fact, according to a news report in 2013,

Russia in an effort to promote the Winter Olympics that the nation was hosting in Sochi, started a drive at its metro stations where passengers could buy tickets by simply doing thirty squats.[4] They actually installed machines on which you had to do the squats to get tickets. Interestingly, the machines were smart enough to tell an incomplete squat from a full squat. See, squats can be rewarding in so many ways.

Pull-ups: Each of us has seen more than enough people hanging from a bar, trying, rather struggling, to pull themselves up while their faces contort out of shape and their legs flail about in hope of helping. My favourite part is the excuses people come up with for being extremely poor at this exercise. They blame it on their weight, weak arms (often despite doing several hundred bicep curls); once someone even reasoned it with a fear of heights!

Well, truth be told, pull-ups are difficult. The only way you can master this exercise is by giving up on excuses and practising till you get it right.

This exercise mainly works your back muscles— one of the bigger muscles in humans. It also engages your lats, core, shoulders and arms. The inside-close

---

4 Andrew Bender, 'Moscow Subway Station Lets Passengers Pay Fare In Squats', *Forbes*, November 14 2013, https://www.forbes.com/sites/andrewbender/2013/11/14/moscow-subway-station-lets-passengers-pay-fare-in-squats/#22c9092cb0d8

grip pull-up is, in fact, better for your arms than the overhyped bicep curls.

You can check the form and variations of pull-ups in the pictorial exercise index. But remember, if your chin doesn't reach over the bar, it's not a valid pull-up. Your target has to be able to get your chest to the bar. Have patience with pull-ups, that's the key.

Push-ups: Salman Khan did it with just one hand in the film *Maine Pyar Kiya*. Van Damme and Sylvester Stallone did the clapping version. This is one exercise everyone uses to show off. You may not consciously know it, but you have been doing some sort of push-ups whenever you lie down on your belly, face down and then get up. Notice how you push yourself up with your arms. But many people struggle with it the moment they have to do it as an exercise. There are easier versions where you are on your knees instead of toes or you change the gradient from 180 degrees to a more convenient angle to push your body up against gravity using your arms, i.e., lean against the wall rather than being perpendicular to the floor. If you belong to the other end of the spectrum and want to make it more challenging, you can increase the gradient by resting your legs on a bench. Yet again, you will find this exercise in the pictorial guide.

Push-ups are the first step to getting a chiselled chest. These are also surprisingly good for the triceps. Apart from being a strength exercise, they are also a great workout to improve your balance and stability.

Dead lift: One of the most practical exercises ever. This one is based purely on your day-to-day actions. Whether it is a pen or a bag or a bucket, you have to pick things up from the ground. Or if you are at the airport, more often than not, you are going to have to lift your bags off the conveyor belt. The dead lift is based on this very action and ensures that you do this the right way, besides giving you a strong back, hamstrings, quadriceps, hips, glutes and core. It also activates your trapezes (shoulders).

You've probably already seen a great demo of a dead lift. Think back to an instance when you saw workers at a construction site lifting heavy objects and material. The back is squeezed, arched upwards, the chest is out and up, the feet are shoulder width apart and the knees are slightly bent. In one swift move, the workers lift the load. Also check the pictures that follow for the correct form and range of

---

Workout No. 2

For time
Three to five rounds:
25 jumping jacks
10 squats
25 high knees
10 push-ups

motion. Be very careful while doing dead lifts because poor form and heavy weights could combine to cause a potentially permanent injury to your back. Do not attempt very heavy weights till you perfect your form. This is one of my favourite exercises because despite its simplicity, a dead lift is a full body workout and leaves me charged with energy.

Also, for the millions who sit in front of their computers for hours together five to six days a week and have a niggling backache that is the cause of constant discomfiture, dead lifts are the cure. Your back and you are going to be very happy once you incorporate this exercise into your life.

Sit-ups: This is one exercise you will like. I probably won't even have to motivate you to do this. Chances are that of all the exercises I have talked about till now, this is the only one you have been doing at home. You call it ab crunches. That, I am afraid, is half a sit-up. Unlike crunches, in which you slightly lift you upper back and head off the floor and then go back down, in a sit-up you come up all the way and, as the name suggests, well, sit up.

This exercise is exclusively for your core—abs and lower back. If your body fat percentage is lower than average, you will soon see lines appearing, also known as the much sought-after abs. Many gym instructors get people to do this or the crunches because their clients keep pestering them for abs. Let me bust a myth here. Sit-ups and crunches do not attack the fat around your belly; their primary goal is to tone and strengthen the core muscles. So, even though you may not have a six-pack, you could have a very strong core if you do enough sit-ups.

Burpees: This is going to be fun. Fun if you are watching someone attempt burpees for the first time. In fact, burpees are quite the rage, almost a fashion statement, across all gyms. So, you will probably get your share of laughs quite easily.

There is not a part of the body that remains unused while doing burpees. It is a compound exercise that involves multiple movements and is as good a cardiovascular exercise as it is for strength training. This is also one of the most-hated exercises, and for that very reason those who show up late for workout sessions at my gym, as well as many others around the world, are made to do burpees as punishment. For a burpee, you need to start from a standing position. From there, bend down and place your palms on the floor near your feet and then jump throwing your feet back so that you are in a plank position. Now, drop your body to the floor, face down. Do a push-up and get back into plank position. From here, jump to bring your feet forward next to your hands. As you stand upright again jump and clap your hands over head. There, that's one burpee. Apart from working the entire body, burpees are also good for burning fat. So, twenty burpees for every cold one you down or the dessert you eat is a good rule to go by.

Lunges: Now, this exercise is slightly different from the ones discussed so far. While all the others included movements that activate several muscle groups and areas of the body at once, lunges mainly work your legs. Yes, they are also good for some core conditioning and stability, but the primary gain is to the quadriceps and thighs. Yet, I treat this as one of the basic exercises in one's armour because it really strengthens your lower body with minimum risk. To introduce a cardiovascular element to this, you could do walking lunges. Those who do lunges regularly add weights once they are comfortable with their body weight. The one thing you would want to keep in mind while doing lunges, with or without weights, is that your front knee should always be in line with the ankle and shouldn't overshoot the toes.

The benefits of lunges include an ability to effortlessly climb up flights of stairs, walk up a slope with ease, better and stronger running, more fire power in the quads for cycling, and, if you are one of those who kick-starts one of those classic old-time motorcycles such as a Royal Enfield Bullet, Jawa or Yezdi Roadking, it will seem like child's play once you join the lunge club.

Push-press: In most countries, air travellers tend to carry much more than the permissible limit of seven kilograms as hand baggage. Again, most passengers struggle to put their heavy bags in the overhead compartment. As is the case more often than not, an air hostess or a steward, who is seasoned at putting away these cumbersome bags, steps in to help and deposits them in their rightful place with a smile in exchange for a feeble 'thank you'.

You won't have to undergo this embarrassment if you ensure that your hand baggage isn't stuffed way beyond what you can handle. Or, if you insist on continuing to push your luck with the airline staff and travel heavy, start doing the push-press. It's a very simple exercise. As the name suggests, you push a weight or a heavy object that's in your hands above your head and then press it up till your elbows straighten out.

This is the only exercise on this list, with the exception of the dead lift, that cannot be done without an accessory. But it's so vital and basic that I feel everyone needs to practise this as often as possible. Don't worry if you don't have dumb-bells, kettlebells or barbells and weights. You can do this with bottles filled with water or sand, your back-pack, your young nephew or niece (only if the parents permit) or stones in the park, as long as you can handle the weight. This exercise involves two distinct movements—the push and the press. The weight rests in your hands with the elbows bent and the palms facing upwards at shoulder level. You bend your legs sixty to seventy degrees at the knees and push your butt back. Now, the push starts from your legs and the momentum thus built moves upwards and you press the weight above your head, extending your arms completely and locking the elbows overhead. Keep at it and you will soon have those broad, muscular shoulders that topless male models flaunt on advertising hoardings across the country.

These eight exercises will help you start off your fitness journey. For the first couple of months, we will plan our workouts with just these movements. We will do different combinations, try out variations and perform these exercises for varying periods of time for now. Once you are confident and comfortable with these, we shall move our game up a notch or two.

Yes, I am aware that you have probably done these exercises in the past and were not happy with the results. That's because you were either focusing on just one body part at a time, or the combination of exercises you did was not enough to push your body, or it just wasn't intense enough to achieve the results you desired. My approach is different from what you may have done in the past. It's going to be intense, varied and new every time you work out. It's going to be interesting, and despite being the same old exercises that didn't work for you, the way we do them now will get you results. These workouts will leave you with no time to check out your vain self in the mirror after every set. At best, you will have just enough time for a sip of water or to catch your breath while moving from one exercise to another. Focus and intensity is the name of the game here. Be prepared.

You might wonder when you'll know you are ready to take things to the next level. For that, you will have to learn to be aware of the signals that your body sends out and also be able to decode these.

For now, let's go back to what fitness is.

Six-pack abs? Maybe. In this day and age of liposuction, plastic surgery, image consciousness and metrosexuality, silicone might be more responsible for washboard abs than exercise and diet. Silicone has enhanced not only women's assets but also men's chests and eight-pack abs. In any case, six-pack abs are just one, not the sole, indicator of fitness.

In fact, you can be fat and fit. A 2008 study conducted at the Centers for Disease Control and Prevention in USA found that people who are overweight, but not obese, had a lower risk of dying from a range of diseases than people with normal weight as calculated by Body Mass Index (BMI).[5]

---

[5] www.cdc.gov

In 2013, scientists from the German Institute of Human Nutrition and the University of Tubingen published a paper in *The Lancet*[6] after studying data from tens of thousands of individuals from across the world, which concluded that one in four of those categorized as obese are fat but fit. They had normal blood pressure levels and the ability to process blood sugar easily. At the metabolic level, they were as fit and healthy as their slimmer counterparts.

On the flipside, we have all heard horror tales about extremely fit athletes facing health problems not caused by injuries. English football club Bolton Wanderer's player Fabrice Muamba suffered a heart attack in the middle of a FA Cup game against Tottenham Hotspurs in 2012. He was just twenty-three then. He was lucky that the medical staff on the pitch was able to resuscitate him, which allowed him to return to a normal life. He was fit as a fiddle, as is expected of top-flight footballers who perform at the highest level week after week. Yet, this man sporting well-defined muscles, strong bones, gifted with speed, single-digit body fat percentage and six-pack abs suffered a heart attack.

---

[6] Prof. Norbert Stefan et al, 'Metabolically Healthy Obesity: Epidemiology, Mechanisms, and Clinical Implications', vol. 1, no. 2, pp. 152–162, (October 2013), *The Lancet*

The aforementioned points are here for a reason. I want to drive home the message that size and fitness have nothing to do with each other. Don't be judgemental and impatient with yourself or others if the weighing scale or the trousers you have been trying to fit into are not indicating the results you desired yet. The important thing is that when you are fit, you will feel it, and soon enough will look like it too.

Since there is no set empirical scale to measure fitness, and the definition of 'fit' is extremely subjective, you may find yourself faced with the simple, yet baffling, question: How fit do I need to be before I can call myself a fit person?

The answer to that question lies in our past, all the way back to our ancestors who lived between 7500 BC and 2000 BC. It was during these years that humans made the transition from being hunters and gatherers to farmers. Our ancestors were so healthy that they could have wrestled us to the ground, slung us over their shoulders and walked away. Even with them carrying a full-grown adult, we would have never been able to catch up with them. This latest research comes from Cambridge University's Dr Colin Shaw who is working with the phenotypic adaptability, variation and evolution research group. 'Even our most highly trained athletes pale in comparison to these ancestors of yours,' Dr Shaw had said in an interview to the fitness magazine

Outside.[7] Shaw's colleague and a PhD candidate at Cambridge, Alison Macintosh, studied the bones of our ancestors and compared her findings with Shaw's study of bone rigidity among present-day Cambridge undergraduates. She found that the ability among male farmers to move about their environment 7300 years ago was, on an average, at a level close to that of our student cross-country runners. The study blames the dip in our strength on technological development, which has made people less active. This decrease in activity has led to a decline in bone density, dip in fitness, obesity, and several other physical and health problems. If we consider our farming and hunter-gatherer ancestors as one end of the fitness spectrum, we can hold on the other end my neighbour, a seventy-five-year-old uncleji who can climb two floors five times a day, without a walking stick, comfortably. Now, depending on your goals, you could aspire for the elite fitness of our ancestors or the functional fitness of my neighbour. The choice is yours. Your body is a machine, it can do anything.

You could easily subject yourself to a few fitness tests by doing some tasks that you may be required

---

[7] Devon Jackson, 'How Far Fitness Has Fallen', *Outside*, April 26 2014, https://www.outsideonline.com/1923776/how-far-fitness-has-fallen

to do in your life. You can know whether you are fit if you can:

1. Push your car to the nearest petrol pump (up to a kilometre away) without asking for help.
2. Lift another average-sized person and walk 100 metres without dropping him/her.
3. Lift a bucket of water from the society tap to your house.
4. Push a punctured bike to the nearest garage up to two kilometres away.
5. Shift furniture at home without having to depend on anyone.
6. Carry your bags from the train station to the taxi.

So, where do you think you stand?

Workout No. 3

Five rounds for one minute each
Push-ups
Sit-ups
Squats
Burpees
Rest

2

Foundations

Aamir Khan had called for me.

I was nervous. What was it about? I had no idea, but I was excited.

I had worked in films and with film stars before. But this was the meticulous Mr Khan. I could hardly sleep that night, wondering what it could be about. I ran through the most inane questions in my mind. 'Should I act like my normal self and go there in my workout vest and tracks, or should I put on a pair of denims and a T-shirt?' There was too much excitement, and my brain was working overtime. A variety of thoughts kept doing somersaults and burpees in my head.

I was also worried about being late. After all, Aamir Khan is known to be very punctual. Considering I punish everyone who shows up late for workouts with ten to twenty burpees, I was afraid to find out what Aamir Khan's punishment might be. I got there with time to spare. It was a two-minute meeting. He knew what he wanted. He wanted to start training with me.

Bollywood legend has it that Aamir, the conscientious man that he is, doesn't do anything or meet anyone until he has done his research. You might spot Saif Ali Khan, John Abraham, Bipasha Basu or other Bollywood stars at popular gyms, but not Aamir. What he wants, he researches and then gets it on his own terms (as far as possible). He didn't waste time—his or mine. He knew what CrossFit was.

Back then, in 2010, he didn't know me though. My younger brother, Kirnay, fondly called Bunny by the family, was an assistant director on Aamir's film *Talaash*. One day, Kirnay showed up on the sets wearing a black sweatshirt with *CrossFit* printed in white across the chest. At the end of the shoot (or maybe sometime during a break), Aamir asked Kirnay about it. The good brother that he is, Kirnay briefly explained what CrossFit was and added that I ran a CrossFit gym in Mumbai. 'He is the CrossFit guy of Mumbai,' he said referring to me. Well, his playing me up in that manner clicked. Aamir asked him to set up a meeting. The next thing I knew, we—Aamir and I—were training together.

Now, Aamir is a very, very fit bloke. We have seen his chiselled body in *Dangal* and *Ghajini*.

Before that, we saw him as a boxer in *Ghulam*. He trains with the best in the business. If you ever want to meet a fit Bollywood actor, Aamir is your man. With the amount of knowledge he has about various exercises and training regimens, he could easily become one of the most informed fitness experts in the country.

We started training while Aamir was shooting for *Talaash*. At that point, he was also preparing for his role as a circus entertainer in *Dhoom 3*. Since the movie involved trapeze performances and a lot of gymnastics, Aamir had already started preparing with his trainer and was taking gymnastics lessons with a personal coach. To me, his brief was simple: teach me how to pull off a handstand, do handstand walks, and keep me in shape.

Aamir trained with me for two months. Around the time we started, he had put on some weight. But he was dedicated and willing to do whatever I asked of him. By the end of two months, he was doing extremely advanced exercises, which included handstand push-ups and handstand walks. You could see his abs, the cuts were well-defined, and all the unwanted fat and weight had disappeared to reveal a well-proportioned body with rippling lean muscles. But ask him and he will tell you that those two months were not a cakewalk. We not only worked on his exercise regimen, but also had to concentrate on nutrition and diet. Since it was Aamir, who questions everything, I had to work very hard to convince him to try new things and switch to the Paleo diet, which I shall discuss in a subsequent chapter. This book is as much for women who are looking to become fit—not skinny and thin enough to squeeze into a size zero dress but *fit*—as it is for men chasing the elusive six-pack while guzzling down an occasional six-pack. If you are one of those for whom the weighing scale is the ultimate indicator of fitness, you really need to rethink your entire concept of fitness. This book will help you do precisely that.

Among Bollywood actresses, I have worked extensively with Jacqueline Fernandes and Sonakshi Sinha. Both are polar opposites as far as body types go. Jacqueline is an established dancer who is extremely fit, athletic and energetic. She is petite, light on her feet and pretty strong for her built.

Sonakshi, on the other hand, doesn't have the typical Bollywood body. Her bone structure and body frame are large, which she can do nothing about. But she certainly could have done a lot about the muscle and tissues connected to her large frame. She has the body type that needs constant exercise to stay in the shape she flaunted in *Dabangg* and subsequent films. If her discipline, diet or workouts lapse for a prolonged period of time, the extra kilos and layers will appear before she knows it. She is dedicated and works very hard, which is why she is as fit as she is. When she came to me, she had spent very little time in the gym. With her, I had to spend much more time working on form and posture so as to make her go through the entire range of exercises.

Though Aamir, Sonakshi and Jacqueline are three very different people with different physiological compositions and needs, all three had to do one common thing—start with the basics.

Basics First

Fitness is a complex and complicated entity. Getting a body like Aamir's in *Dhoom 3* or *Ghajini* is not simple. It's not as if you start working out and the fat starts dissipating, muscles start getting bigger and more defined, and you begin looking lean and beefed-up. It takes much more than that. Discipline, diet and dedication are the three holy pillars of fitness. Ignore any one and you may be better off than where you started but still won't be as fit as you could have been, or wanted to be. You won't see the results that you had imagined: a body like Aamir Khan's, the ripped physique of Sylvester Stallone in *Rambo* and Daniel Craig as James Bond, or a beautifully proportioned shell like Scarlet Johansson, Jennifer Lawrence or Jacqueline Fernandes.

Let's begin with the basics. That is where Aamir, Jacqueline and Sonakshi started. That is where everyone else started. Leave your ego behind and go back to the A, B, C of fitness no matter how much you may have advanced in the gym. This is going to be integral in laying the foundations of your fitness journey.

Aamir is fit and strong and exercises regularly. The fact that he questioned everything and went deep into whatever he undertook meant that he was already aware of the movements involved in working out with me, which are integral to the eight basic exercises we covered in the previous chapter. So with him, the foundation work was easy. But he went through this process too. Just that it was done quicker than usual. It was pretty smooth sailing with Jacqueline as well, while with Sonakshi I had to go slow because of her body type and inexperience. But she is a fast learner who mastered all the movements just a week into training.

By foundation I mean the basic movements and concepts of exercise, using which you can build your workout regimen in order to achieve your fitness goals. These movements are pull, push and hold.

The basic exercises are squats, pull-ups, push-ups, sit-ups, burpees, planks or bridge holds and lunges. Since push-press requires weights, we shall include that at a later stage after you have undergone some amount of conditioning.

Everyone starts with these exercises, minus the barbells, dumb-bells, kettlebells or any other weight. Once you are convinced that your form is right, you can move on to adding weights to your exercise regimen. But before you start forming the misguided notion that lifting more weight is the only sign of being fit, try running 10 kilometres in less than sixty minutes (a comfortable target for close to 45 per cent of the population) or do the basic CrossFit routine of five pull-ups, ten push-ups and twenty squats for twenty minutes non-stop. At the end of the run or the twenty minutes, you will realize how beneficial these exercises are for your muscular, cardiovascular and core fitness as well as endurance. Free-hand exercise is just as important as lifting weights: this is one of the basic principles of fitness that many trainers seem to gloss over in their pursuit of giving their clients pumped up or size-zero bodies really quickly. If you are just starting out, stick to body weight movements and try to do three to five rounds of each exercise with ten repetitions in the beginning. Gradually move up to fifteen and twenty repetitions over the course of two weeks. Also, in the initial phase, pick only three to four movements for your workout for a day. Before you start, check the proper way to perform the exercises with help from the pictorial guide in the book.

Warm-up (Yes, you have heard this before)

You can't shock your body into lifting a 100-kg barbell all of a sudden, or break into a 13-second sprint out of the blue without pulling a muscle or two. So, even before you start the basic exercises, you need to stretch, mobilize and warm-up. Your joints, muscles and bones need to be prepared for the workout ahead. I like to call it the Fitness Foreplay. Its nature and duration depend entirely on what workout you have planned for the day.

What is stretching?

We all know what stretching is. All of us do it, knowingly or involuntarily, irrespective of whether we work out or not. We have seen, and will continue to see, cricketers, footballers and all other

---

Workout No. 4

Five rounds each:
25 V-ups
25 hollow rocks
25 back extensions
25 crunches

sportspersons do it on our television screens and in stadiums whenever we go for some live action. We even see our dogs and cats do it. So much so that they have named stretches after our favourite pets: downward dog, cat-camel, bird-dog, to name a few.

I want you to understand the science behind stretching and the reason we need to do so before a workout.

If you were to break into a full-blooded 100-metre sprint like a bolt from the blue or, better still, like Usain Bolt, or if you walk into the gym and go straight for five dead lifts with 100-kg weights, there are high chances that you will pull a muscle or hurt yourself.

That's because you can't jump-start your muscles and tendons with high intensity activities. All your body gets is a rude shock, pulled muscles, displaced joints, or worse.

If you spend even five minutes stretching, blood flow to the extremities increases, as does oxygen supply to the muscle tissues being engaged in the activity. According to a paper published in the *Strength and Conditioning Journal* in December 1999, stretching leads to a spike in intramuscular temperature which 'reduces the likelihood of muscle, connective tissue, or ligamentous damage by enhancing tissue elasticity. Elevated muscle temperature also increases the muscles' ability to tolerate stresses with a reduced level of strain'.[1]

But before you get carried away, you should know that extreme stretching can also potentially injure you, even before you begin your workout. Pre-exercise stretching, points out researcher Ian Shrier at McGill University in Montreal and former president of the Canadian Academy of Sports Medicine, can easily take muscles into the damage range.[2] When the task is approached with the excessive determination shown by many enthusiasts, damage is almost guaranteed.

The muscles that need maximum stretching are the bigger ones: hamstrings, quadriceps, calves, glutes, back, neck, chest, and shoulders.

So, find your balance and gear up to move on to the next stage—mobility.

What is mobility?

While stretching increases blood flow and oxygen supply to the muscles, mobility exercises free up the

[1] Gesztesi et al, 'Stretching During Exercise,' *Strength & Conditioning Journal* (199), vol. 21, no. 6, p. 44 http://journals.lww.com/nsca-scj/Citation/1999/12000/Stretching_During_Exercise.10.aspx

[2] Ian Shrier, 'Should People Stretch Before Exercise?' *Western Journal of Medicine* (2001), vol. 174(4), pp. 282–83, https://www.ncbi.nlm.nih.gov/pmc/articles/PMC1071358/

joints so as to ensure that your body can go through the full range of the workout. Stretching only focuses on lengthening short and tight muscles, explains one of the world's leading mobility coach and author of the *New York Times* bestseller *Becoming a Supple Leopard*, Kelly Starrett.[3]

Mobility, on the other hand, refers to the range of motions the body and joints are capable of. If the muscles around the joints are stiff, or if you have flexibility issues, your mobility is compromised with and you cannot go through the complete range of motions that is necessary for any exercise to be effective. According to the American Council for Exercise (ACE), mobility is 'the degree to which an articulation (where two bones meet) is allowed to move before being restricted by surrounding tissues (ligaments/tendons/muscles, etc.), which is otherwise known as the range of uninhibited movement around a joint.'

According to Starrett, mobilization is a movement-based integrated full-body approach that addresses all the elements that limit movement and performance, including short and tight muscles, soft tissue restriction, joint capsule restriction, motor control problems, joint range of motion dysfunction,

---

[3] *Real Insurance*, 'Why Mobility Is Important To Runners', 10 May 2017, https://www.realinsurance.com.au/news-views/why-mobility-is-important-to-runners

and neural dynamic issues. In short, mobilization is a tool to address movement and performance problems.

Just like we go through stretching and warm-up routines before starting any workout, mobilizing our joints and the muscles around them is another drill we need to go through in order to improve our performance.

Mobility is a fairly new addition to the world of exercise. So, if the trainers at your neighbourhood gym haven't heard of it, don't be surprised. Several established athletes and bodybuilders also might not have heard of this term.

However, now that you know, and as the human body is capable of things that you cannot even imagine, let's include some mobility workouts to get you the body or the fitness levels that you have often pictured for yourself.

Some of the most common mobility exercises open up not only the big joints but also the smaller muscle groups that are crucial to the exercises.

For example, before doing squats, you not only need to work on your hips and ankles, but also on your calves. Tight ankles or calves can restrict your squatting movement, just as much as tight hips can. Before doing push-ups, bench presses or shoulder presses, you will have to ensure that your thoracic spine (commonly called the T-spine or upper back) and glenohumeral joints (the ball and socket joints in the shoulders) have complete range of motion so as to be able to not only go through the full exercise movement but also be stable at the end when the weights are directly above you with your elbows extended. The other main groups that need to be stable or moving freely in order to workout effectively are the pelvis, lumbar spine and scapulo-thoracic joint, the spot where the scapula meet the thorax.

The exercises that you should be doing are:

1. Ankle mobility: Start by standing on your heels with your forefoot off the ground and then slowly rock forward, shifting all your weight to the toes while lifting your heels.
2. Walking hip openers: Lift your leg with the knee bent at 90 degrees and then move it out as far as you can, ending up in an open stance. Then bring it back in slowly, put your foot down and do the same with the other leg.
3. T-spine mobility movements: Hang from a pull-up bar with a wide grip, ask a friend to put his/her palms on the small of your back, and push, gradually moving upwards along the spine towards the nape.
4. Scapular push-ups for glenohumeral mobility: Go into a plank either on your elbows or on your palms. From here, drop the chest down

to let your shoulder blades come together or perform the cat-camel movement in which you are on all fours: pull your stomach in and round your back upwards like a cat stretching itself. Hold this position for five to ten seconds. From here, drop your lower back, arch it as much as you can while raising your neck like a camel. At this point, your shoulder blades will come together.

Now that you have stretched and mobilized, the next thing you need to do is warm-up for the main workout.

What is warm-up?

Warm-up is the part where you start preparing your musculoskeletal structure, or your body, by putting it through movements similar to the exercises that you plan to do during your workout. The main aim of the warm-up is to slowly and gradually load the muscle groups that will be activated during the workout. So, planning your warm-up is just as important as planning your workout.

- The good thing about planning the warm-up is that you already have a reference point (the main workout), which makes it easier for you to know what it ought to be. For example, if your workout includes squats, you know you need to warm-up the muscle groups in the lower back, glutes (butt) and legs. So, you could do air squats, which are squats at a higher tempo, or lunges, or box jumps.

- For box jumps, select a height that you can easily jump to. Then find a steady box or platform and jump to land on it with your feet together. Stand up tall and step down or jump down as warm-up. To this, you can add another movement that activates your core, like sit-ups or V sit-ups, and yet another that involves the upper back and shoulder muscles, which will support the weights, like American kettlebell swings (explained in the pictorial guide) or push-ups.

Let me give you a couple of examples of a warm-up routine for a typical workout that you are likely to find in the book.

If the workout is the classic five pull-ups, ten push-ups and twenty squats for twenty minutes, do two rounds of the following:

25 jumping jacks
10 sit-ups
20 high-knees
10 shoulder dislocates

Do some arm, wrist, ankle, neck and hip rotations too.

Say the workout is 21 repetitions of thrusters, 15 of pull-ups, followed by 9 repetitions of both exercises (21-15-9). For this, the warm-up would target muscle groups in the legs, shoulders, core and upper back. It could include three rounds of ten repetitions of burpees, shoulder or push-presses, sit-ups and goblet[4] or air squats.

The intensity and length of the warm-up is also directly dependent on your workout. If you are doing a long or body weight workout, you can get away with a short, quick stretching-mobility-warm-up session. But if you are doing a short and heavy routine, you need to spend more time on preparing your body for the intense workload ahead.

Now, you are ready to work out.

---

[4] A goblet squat is done by holding one dumb-bell or kettlebell in your hands at chest level.

3

Work Out like a Boss

'Will you be doing an upper body or lower body routine today?'

I often hear this remark in gyms—even the popular and reputed ones—both in India and abroad.

Each time, I feel bewildered and ask myself: What are they talking about?

When things get steamy with your partner, do you ask each other: Will you be doing the upper body or lower body routine today? Obviously not. You want to work on the whole deal. So, when it comes to working out, why would you want to work on just one part of the body at a time?

Workout No. 5

EMOM for 20 mins (1 min rest after every five rounds)
25 mountain climbers,
10 push-ups

After all my years of training and coaching, I am grateful to CrossFit and functional fitness for one thing—it helped me realize the importance of getting all parts of my body involved while designing a workout routine, no matter how long or short it may be.

One might argue the importance of isolation workouts. Isolation exercises focus on engaging one body part at a time. Even that can be easily weaved into your exercise regimen if you plan smartly. However, if you are looking at bodybuilding, then the approach will be very different from what we are dealing with here. In this book, the attempt is to help you achieve overall fitness. This particular chapter will show you how to plan your daily workout, what athletes mean by active recovery and illustrate with photographs some of the basic exercises that you will need to perform often. Also included here is a glossary of all exercises, which, together with the pictures, should help you plan your workouts. If you would prefer to follow the set workouts that the others and I follow at my gyms, an extensive workout directory has also been provided at the end. I hope you have been doing the exercises mentioned on every tenth page till now.

How to plan your workout?

The major muscle groups in the upper body are chest, shoulders and upper back while those in the lower body are legs, butt and lower back. Digging deeper into human physiology, in layman's terms, the upper body's smaller muscle groups are the biceps, triceps, forearms, lats and traps, which are a part of your shoulders, connecting to the neck on either side. In the lower body, the muscles in the legs are hamstrings, quadriceps and calves while the butt consists of glutes or the gluteus muscles.

While planning your workout, no matter what the duration or intensity, you must design it in such a way that the major muscle groups in both the upper and lower body are engaged to a certain degree. Just think of the time you hiked up a mountain. Though it was your legs and butt doing most of the work, without core strength and strong arms you probably wouldn't have made it past that rock in the middle of your path that made you pull yourself up using your arms and engaging your shoulders. Never do you do things with just one half of your body; it is always the complete body that is involved.

To illustrate my point, let's take an exercise like weighted back squats as an example, which are typically considered a part of the lower back routine. If you haven't perfected the squat without weights, do not try this. You will know you are ready for a weighted back squat when you are able to do twenty squats with relative ease. The starting position for the weighted back squat is with you standing upright, the weight-bearing barbell resting on your shoulders and your arms bent at the elbows, gripping the barbell. As you start lowering yourself into the squat, the glutes and hamstrings get engaged, but even before that you unconsciously activate your core by controlling your breathing and pulling the stomach in. The grip on the barbell gets tighter as you descend and is the tightest at the bottom or the end position of the squat. As you come up, your quadriceps and hamstrings work hard while the arms push up and the core provides balance. At the end of the set, you will not only find all the major muscles in your legs pumped up but also your biceps. This is besides slight fatigue in the lower back. So, when you use your whole body for almost anything you do, why would you train just one half on a given day?

In our fast-paced lives, we need to make the most of whatever time we can manage after work, family time, social media and outings. So, when I plan an exercise routine for my clients or myself, I aim to get in a complete body workout, even if the focus is on one specific movement that engages a certain body part or muscle group more than others.

In most gyms, people would hear terms like push and pull movements. It is true that most exercises can be classified under these two broad categories, but instead of figuring out which exercises come under which, we shall take a slightly different approach to planning your daily workouts initially. The strategy is to pick one exercise for the upper body, one for the lower body and one for the core. So, in the initial weeks when you aren't using weights, if you choose to do push-ups, it takes care of the upper body. Then you could pick squats for the lower body and sit-ups for the core. The next day it could be pull-ups (upper body), walking lunges (lower body) and leg raises (core).

If you are one of those who couldn't indulge in a sport once you left college and got sucked into what we call life—career, society, family— and have finally found the time to take care of yourself, then start slow. It is not etched in stone that you have to do ten repetitions of each of the three exercises you have chosen. If ten repetitions seem too easy for one exercise, go ahead and do twenty so that you feel your muscle groups getting engaged. This is frequently true of simple exercises such as jumping jacks, high knees, step-ups, etc. On the opposite end of the exercise spectrum, you will find that you struggle with pull-ups, especially when you ensure that your chin is level with the bar you are suspended from. So, for this, do just three repetitions to start with. Somewhere in between you will find movements like push-ups, sit-ups and squats, for which ten reps are challenging enough, so stick to that number. Slowly, over time, you will build on your fitness and your body will start getting used to the rigour of more strenuous workouts. To be able to get to that stage, you should look at adding two reps every week to each of the exercises you struggled with till you reach the count of ten. For exercises that you find easy, try and get comfortable with performing thirty to forty reps. Do twenty reps for exercises that you could hit the magic number of ten at the beginning.

If you have already done your math and see yourself reaching from three to ten pull-ups in just a month or a little over that, reality is most likely to hit you. Once you get to the stage where you can do seven to eight pull-ups, progress will be slow. You might take two to three weeks to move forward. But don't lose heart or be hard on yourself, this is normal. Progress slows as you inch closer to the peak.

A week or so after you can do ten pull-ups together, you will find yourself confident enough to start using weights with almost all exercises. However, chances are that you would have already felt confident enough to start introducing weights for simpler movements. There is no harm if you have already done that. But, after you are at a level where you can do all weight-bearing exercises, make a conscious effort to work harder on the movements you were weaker in. The load-bearing exercises that you ought to stick to for now are the simple ones, such as front and back squats, dead lifts, bench presses, shoulder/military presses, upright rows or high-pulls, bent-over rows and lunges.

For the next two to four weeks, follow the principle of progressive loading and gradually increase the weight you use for each exercise. It is best to maintain a diary to record how many reps you manage at different weights. This will help you track progress. The ideal number of reps during the initial stages of weight training is ten per movement; you can progressively increase the load over the next six weeks or so. By this time, you should be plateauing. You should start reducing the number of reps to seven while increasing the load. Continue increasing it till such time that you can do no more than five reps of each movement.

Keep in mind that you may take a little more or less time than specified here, as everyone has different levels of fitness and takes to exercise at a different pace.

Once you introduce weights into your workouts, you could move to complex exercises such as squat cleans, thrusters, weighted squats, overhead squats, dead lifts, push press, clean and press, clean and jerk, split jerk, kettlebell swings, high pulls and snatches. To aid understanding, each movement is explained in detail with pictures. Almost all of these exercises engage muscle groups in both the upper and lower body. So, you could do a two-part workout, the first focusing on skill or strength, and the second to get your body working at an elevated heart rate over a certain period of time, or to exercise your entire body. Since the first part is about strength or skill, the pace of the workout should be slow with enough time for recovery, while the weight should be on the heavier side. For the second part, the focus has to be on speed and endurance, so go easy with the weights. A typical workout for this could be one set of five weighted squats every two minutes for ten minutes at increasing weights, followed by a ten-minute break. The second part could include performing five power cleans, ten box jumps and fifteen sit-ups continuously for twenty minutes with as little rest as possible between sets. Here, again, your aim should be to get a full body workout.

I had mentioned earlier in the chapter that you could plan a full body workout even with the more common weight exercises such as bench presses, bent-over rows, upright rows, shoulder presses, etc. which are practised and preached widely in most gyms. Since it is the principle of isolation that you are falling back on here, the focus has to be on strength. Your workout could look something like this: five bench presses and five bent-over rows at increasing weights, five sets with thirty to sixty seconds rest between each exercise. This can be followed by five back squats, five lunges, both at increasing weights, five sets with thirty to sixty seconds rest between each exercise. You could then do ten bicep curls, ten skull crushers, three sets at increasing weights with thirty to sixty seconds of rest. Also, you could do five sets of fifteen sit-ups and one-minute plank holds. Once you learn all the movements demonstrated here, any number of workout permutations and combinations are possible to ensure you are never bored. The other advantage is that the workout is always something exciting, which means your muscles are constantly adapting and becoming stronger.

One last thing that you need to remember while planning a workout is *rest*. If your muscles do not recover and you still sweat it out in the gym or the park, all you would be doing is harming them, not building them. You need to have one day of complete rest while another day has to be set aside for active recovery. While complete rest should ideally be at the end of the week so that you start again with fresh muscles, there should be an active recovery day in the middle of the week. Active recovery is when you work on the tired muscles and joints to relieve them of the stress by doing a very light workout. This can include easy jogging, cycling, swimming, stretching, physiotherapy, massage, meditation and foam-rolling.

Foam-rolling, physiotherapy and massages are very crucial for your muscles to remain flexible, strong and fatigue-free. While foam-rolling is something you can do yourself in the gym or at home, massage and physiotherapy require expert intervention. For foam-rolling, you need a simple foam roller that is readily available at sports and fitness stores as well as online. To use it, lay the roller on the floor and place the affected region (such as the front of the thighs, hamstrings, back) on top of it. Then move your body up and down and sideways for at least thirty to sixty seconds. This will let the roller massage the affected areas. For massage and physiotherapy, try and pick a sports massage therapist or a physiotherapist who understands an active person's needs better and can provide relief as well as ensure you remain free of injuries.

As for stretching, if you are the kind who feels that stretching is a waste of time, there are other ways to lengthen and relax your tense muscles. One of the best ways to do so is to practise yoga once or twice a week.

Now, you are ready to roll.

Workout No. 6

Three to five rounds each:
10 burpees
15 squats
20 push-ups
25 sit-ups
30 high knees

4

Exercise Glossary

- **Squat cleans:** This is one of the basic movements to learn for Olympic and powerlifting. The word 'clean' is used to refer to a movement where we pull a barbell, dumb-bell, kettlebell, medicine ball or any other weight off the floor and bring it up to the shoulders. In a squat clean, one must pull the weight up from the floor to the shoulder using proper technique and simultaneously perform a squat by getting underneath the weight. This is a great way to lift heavier weights.
- **Thrusters:** These can be performed with barbells, kettlebells or dumb-bells at shoulder level while you are in a standing position. In case you are using a barbell, ensure that it rests on your shoulder blades. Starting from a standing position, go down into a squat and then swiftly stand back up using the momentum to push the

weight in your hands above your head with your arms fully stretched and elbows locked out.

- **Overhead squats:** Holding the barbell in a wide grip above your head with arms fully extended and elbows locked out, lower yourself towards the floor, pushing your butt back and knees outwards, just like in a normal squat. Then stand back up with the weight above your head all along.

- **Push press:** Start from the standing position with the weight at shoulder level. Bend your knees, push your butt back slightly and then go upwards in one explosive movement. In one swift motion, using the momentum generated by the legs and hips, push the weight above your head, fully extending the arms and locking both elbows out.

- **Clean and press:** In this, the weight is on the floor and you need to pull it up to your shoulders, followed by a push press that ends with the weight overhead and arms fully extended and elbows locked out. There is a short pause after the clean during which you should inhale and prepare for the push press. The heavier the weight, the longer the pause between the clean and press.

- **Clean and jerk:** This is an Olympic lift and is part of all weightlifting competitions. Perform a squat clean off the floor and once you are standing with the barbell on your shoulders, you are ready to perform the jerk. Just like a push press, start by lowering yourself into a quarter squat by bending your knees and pushing your hips back. In one swift motion, push upwards back to the standing position, simultaneously pushing the barbell above your head. Before you extend your arms completely and lock your elbows overhead, get under the weight by splitting one leg backwards and the other forward like a lunge and then lock your elbows out. Bring your feet together in line and come back up to standing position with the weight overhead.

- **Split jerk:** This is the same as 'Clean and Jerk'. Just skip the 'clean' part and start with the weight on your shoulders in front and perform the jerk.
- **Kettlebell swings:** This is how you swing while working out. Stand with your legs two feet apart. Grip a kettlebell with both hands and let your hands hang down the middle. The kettlebell will be just below your groin. Bend your knees slightly and push your hips back in a way that your shoulders move slightly towards the floor. Now push forward with your hips and let the momentum created push the kettlebell in your hands forward. Your arms and the kettlebell form a pendulum, and every time you push the kettlebell forward with your hips it travels up to your shoulder, follows the same trajectory

and falls back towards your hips. When it is at its lowest position, bend your knees and push your hips back so as to let the weight follow its trajectory slightly behind your body, and then again push forward with your hips to start another swing.

- **High-pulls:** This movement is integral to both clean and snatch lifts, which is why it is practised as a separate exercise in order to improve the other two more comprehensive lifts. Stand with your feet hip-width apart and the barbell touching your shins. Hold the bar in a clean or snatch grip and now pull it up to your chest in one swift motion. You must remember to push your elbows wide and keep them pointed towards the ceiling till they are in line with your shoulder. From here, let the weight come down in a controlled motion and set it on the floor to repeat the same movement. This is the high-pull. One thing you need to bear in mind is to use your hips to push the weight up when you reach that height off the floor. This will let you lift heavier weights.

- **Snatch:** Another Olympic lift, the Snatch, when performed with a barbell, is an integral part of all weightlifting competitions. The biggest difference here is that the weight goes from the ground to over your head in one movement unlike the clean and jerk where you pause at the shoulder. The snatch grip is much wider, about 30 inches apart. One way to find out whether the grip is correct is to hold the bar in what you think is the correct position and then bring it up to your waist. If the bar is at the level of your hips where you hinge, then it is correct. Now, starting off the floor, pull the weight upwards and quickly get underneath it. Once it is overhead and your arms are completely extended, lock your elbows and stabilize the weight overhead. From here, stand upright while balancing the weight overhead. Sounds complex? Use YouTube or see any Olympic weightlifting competition online and you will find out just how challenging, yet fun, this lift is.

- **Tabata:** It is a very specific high intensity interval training in which you perform a chosen exercise for twenty seconds followed by ten seconds of rest repeated for eight cycles, which comes up to four very sweaty and exhausting minutes.
- **AMRAP:** As Many Rounds As Possible.
- **Bridge hold:** This is a core-strengthening and stability workout also known as the plank. Lie down on your stomach and then come up to the push-up start position. Squeeze your abs and butt and continue breathing while you hold the position. If doing this on your palms is difficult, you could drop down to your elbows and hold the bridge position here.

- **Hollow hold:** Another core workout to get that chiselled Jason Statham six, or eight, pack. Lie flat on your back and raise your shoulders and legs slightly, without bending your knees and pointing your toes away from you, off the floor and hold them there. Squeeze your abs while doing this and make sure that the hips and lower back are in contact with the ground.
- **Bear crawls:** If you have seen a bear walk on all fours, you know how to do this exercise.
- **Air squats:** Normal squats done without any weights. Make sure you push your knees outwards, hips back and lower yourself till your butt is below parallel to the ground.
- **Box jump:** Select a height that you can easily jump to. Find a steady box or platform and jump with both your feet to land on it. Once you land on the box, stand up tall and step down or jump down.
- **Handstand push-ups:** Start with a headstand and then use your arms to raise yourself up into a handstand. In a controlled manner, lower yourself again to a headstand and then back to a handstand. So, it is just like push-ups but upside down. It looks pretty cool and will definitely turn heads. You can do this against a wall or without any support if you can manipulate the centre of gravity and find the golden balance.

- **Tabata squats:** See Tabata.
- **Tabata push-ups:** See Tabata.
- **Bottom of squat:** The lowest position of the squat where your hips are below parallel to the ground and the knees are pushed outwards.
- **Hollow rock hold:** Same as Hollow Hold.
- **Plebs plank:** Bridge hold at the top of the push-up position.
- **Sumo deadlift high-pulls:** Stand like a Sumo wrestler with your legs about two feet apart pointing sideways in opposite direction and knees bent. Keeping your back straight, bend down and hold the barbell in a narrow or close grip. The first movement you need to learn is the Sumo deadlift. Engage your abs and gluteus muscles and swiftly stand up straight, bringing the weight up as you do so. Your feet and the distance between them must remain fixed. Now, you are ready to perform the Sumo deadlift high-pull. Do everything as instructed in the Sumo deadlift, but this time instead of merely standing up with the weight, pull it up as high as your chest while pointing your elbows upwards like you did for the high-pulls.
- **V-Ups:** A core-strengthening and abs shredding exercise rolled into one movement. Start by lying on your back and arms extended straight behind the head. Now, raise your legs and arms together,

as if closing a book (forming the V shape), and bring your hands to touch your feet right above your waist. Then go back to the starting position.

- **Back extensions:** Lying down on your stomach, plant both your palms on either side of your chest. Now, slowly raise your upper body while engaging your core. Ensure that your stomach stays on the floor. Lower yourself to the starting position slowly and repeat.

- **Max bridge hold:** The maximum duration for which you can hold the bridge or plank position.

- **Max hollow hold:** The maximum amount of time for which you can stay in the hollow hold position.

- **EMONTM:** Every Minute On The Minute.

- **Squat jumps:** This is air squats with a twist, or should I say spring. Instead of merely standing up from the bottom position of the squat, you go on to jump in the air. When your feet are back on the ground, you lower yourself into a squat. This is to be done in one seamless movement.

Workout No. 7

Three rounds (90 seconds work, 30 seconds rest)
Box step-ups
10 high knees + 1 burpee
Suryanamaskar
Bicycle kicks

- **HSPU:** Handstand push-ups.
- **Sandbags clean and press:** Clean and press performed with a duffel bag filled with sand or some other weight.
- **R/L-arm kb (kettlebell) thrusters:** These are thrusters (see above) with a kettlebell in just one hand at a time.
- **Overhead lunges:** Think regular lunges but while holding a weight overhead with your arms fully extended and elbows locked out.
- **Medicine ball cleans:** Cleans that are performed with a medicine ball instead of barbells, dumbbells or kettlebells.
- **Hang power snatch:** 'Hang' in any movement means that you are standing and holding the weight, which hangs around your thighs. The inclusion of the term 'power' in either a clean or a snatch exercise essentially takes the squat movement out of the traditional movements. So, starting from the hang position, dip your knees and push your hips back a bit. Then, in an explosive motion, while coming back to the standing position, pull the weight directly overhead, fully extending your arms and locking your elbows out. Bear in mind that you still have to get under the weight and you can, at the most, bend your knees a little and lower yourself into one-fifth of a squat and not any lower. Come

back to the standing position with the weight steady overhead.

- **Hang power clean:** Start from the hang position and perform the 'Clean' without squatting. Again, you cannot go lower than one-fifth of a squat.
- **Max H(ang) P(ower) clean:** The heaviest weight you can perform the Hang Power Clean with.
- **Wall climbs:** Lie face down on the floor with the soles of your feet touching a wall and your palms on either side of the chest as in the bottom position of a push-up. From here, start moving your feet up the wall and walk backwards with your hands moving towards the wall. The end position of the wall climb is when you are in the handstand position with your hands fully extended and the chest touching the wall. Then, slowly move your hands forward and feet towards the floor, returning to the starting position.
- **C2B pull-ups:** Chest to bar pull-ups. This is a pull-up where you need to pull yourself up till your chest touches, or is close to, the bar you are hanging from.
- **Wall-ball shots:** Stand facing a wall, grab a medicine ball and hold it chest high using both hands and with your elbows pointing towards

the ground. Now, lower yourself into a squat. As you come up, throw the ball overhead on to the wall. Catch the ball as it comes back down and, in the same motion, lower yourself into a squat with the ball in hand. Repeat.

- **Double-unders:** This is just like regular skipping, the only difference being that you have to get the skipping rope to pass under your feet twice in every jump.

- **Supermans:** Lie flat on your stomach and stretch your hands straight beyond your head so that your biceps touch the ears. Now lift your legs and upper body, including the arms, such that only your belly is in contact with the floor. Squeeze your abs and butt and hold for at least 30 seconds. This movement is called the Superman because it looks like you are trying to fly.

- **L-sit hold:** Sit on the floor with your legs stretched in front of you. Make sure your knees don't bend and that your back is perpendicular to the floor. Now, put your palms on the floor and lift your body off the floor such that your butt and legs are off the ground. You abs must be engaged and active at this point.

- **Downward dog:** Lie flat on your stomach and place your palms on the floor. Slowly, push your palms into the floor, bring your feet towards your chest and lift your body by pushing your butt towards the ceiling. Bring your feet as close to the palms as possible without bending your knees. When you can't go any further, hold the position. You will feel a stretch in your hamstrings and lower back.

- **Pistols:** These are one-legged squats. The other leg never touches the ground.

Squats and Air Squats

Raise your arms
to shoulder level.

Pushing your hips back and your knees
outwards, not forward, lower yourself
into a full squat till your butt is below
parallel to the floor.

Keeping your spine straight and
abdominal muscles squeezed, push your
heels firmly into the ground. Get back
up, lowering your arms as you do so.

Side view: Pushing your hips back and
your knees outwards, not forward, lower
yourself into a full squat till your butt is
below parallel to the floor.

Front Squats

Hold the barbell in the front rack position, such that is rests on your shoulders and just above your collar bone, standing upright. Your elbows need to be at shoulder level.

Lower yourself into a squat by pushing your hips back and knees outwards, making sure that the weight continues to rest on your shoulders in the front rack position while your elbows remain parallel to the shoulders.

Get back up to the starting position while keeping your spine straight, abdominal muscles squeezed, heels pushing firmly into the ground and maintaining the front rack position.

Side view: Lower yourself into a squat by pushing your hips back and knees outwards, making sure that the weight continues to rest on your shoulders in the front rack position while your elbows remain parallel to the shoulders.

Overhead Squats

Use a wide grip on the barbell such that when you let your arms hang down with the weight the bar is at the crease of your hips. Now, lift this weight up overhead.

A side view of the starting position for overhead squats. The arms are fully extended, elbows are locked out and the spine is straight.

Holding the weight overhead, squeeze your core and gluteus muscles to stabilize yourself and go down into a squat. Remember, move your hips back and knees out wide. Keeping your feet slightly wider than your shoulder width will help maintain balance.

A side view of the bottom position of the overhead squat. From here, stand up straight holding the weight overhead all the while.

Strict or Military Press

The starting position is the same as the front squat. Standing upright, hold the barbell in the front rack position such that is rests on your shoulders and just above your collar bone. Your elbows should be level with the shoulders.

Using your arms, push the weight directly overhead in a straight line such that your arms are fully extended and the elbows are locked out. You need to be absolutely steady when the weight is overhead.

In a controlled movement, bring the weight down to your shoulders like in the starting position. From here, repeat the exercise.

Side view: Using your arms, push the weight directly overhead in a straight line such that your arms are fully extended and the elbows are locked out. You need to be absolutely steady when the weight is overhead.

Push Press

The starting position is the same as the front squat. Hold the barbell in the front rack position such that is rests on your shoulders and just above your collar bone, standing upright. Your elbows should be level with your shoulders.

Lower your body by pushing your hips backwards and bending your knees slightly. This is called a dip.

Now, with your heels firmly pressed into the floor, use your legs and hips to push upwards so as to straighten your legs out completely. At the same time use the momentum created to push the weight overhead. Perform this movement with speed.

You need to have the weight overhead with your arms stretched out and elbows locked while you stand steady.

Side view of the starting position.

Side view of the dip.

Side view: Now, with your heels firmly pressed into the floor, use your legs and hips to push upwards so as to straighten your legs out completely. At the same time use the momentum created to push the weight overhead. Perform this movement with speed.

Side view of the top position of the push press as well as the strict or military press.

Side view: In a controlled movement, bring the weight back to your shoulders like in the starting position. While receiving the weight on your shoulders, soften the stress on your body by bending your knees slightly. From here, repeat the exercise.

Dead Lifts

Step close to the weight resting on the floor such that the barbell touches your shins. Now, while bending your knees slightly start lowering your chest towards the bar till you can hold it with your hands. That's the starting position of the dead lift. Make sure that your back is not arching and the spine is straight. Also take care not to go into the squat position.

Now, engage your core and while keeping your spine straight and chest up, pull the bar up in a smooth, swift motion as you stand up.

Stand up straight with the weight in your hands around your thighs and clench your gluteus muscles while your spine is remains neutral.

Side view: Starting position of the dead lift.

Side view: Starting position of the dead lift.

Side view: Now, engage your core and while keeping your spine straight and chest up, pull the bar up in a smooth, swift motion as you stand up.

Side view: Stand up straight all the way with the weight in your hands around your thighs and clench your gluteus muscles while your spine remains neutral.

Kettlebell Swings (KBS) Russian style

Stand up straight and hold a kettlebell in your hands with your arms hanging naturally, without bending your elbows or locking them out.

Letting your arms hang naturally with the kettlebell in hand, lean forward with your knees slightly bent.

As you return to the standing position, squeeze your glutes and abs and push the weight with your hips. This will push your arms and weight up towards the ceiling. Let the weight move like a pendulum and go all the way up to your shoulder level.

Let the weight swing upwards like a pendulum till it reaches up to your shoulders.

Now, let the weight move back down like a pendulum. As it reaches your waist, bend your knees slightly and start leaning forward with your chest.

Lean forward so that the weight is back to where it was between your legs as in the second picture. This is to allow you to repeat the movement.

Side view: Let the weight swing upwards like a pendulum till it reaches up to your shoulders.

Kettlebell Swings (KBS) American style

Start just the way you did with the Russian style KBS.

Just like you did with the Russian style KBS, bend your knees slightly, lean forward with the kettlebell in hand and engage your gluteus muscles and core.

Now, as you stand up straight, thrust the weight upwards with your hips. This time, instead of stopping when the weight reaches your shoulders, use some of your arm strength and take the weight all the way over your head.

Side view: Just like you did with the Russian style KBS, bend your knees slightly, lean forward with the kettlebell in hand and engage your gluteus muscles and core.

Side view: Now, as you stand up straight, thrust the weight upwards with your hips. This time, instead of stopping when the weight reaches your shoulders, use some of your arm strength and take the weight all the way over your head.

Side view: Once the weight is directly overhead, let it come down on its own following the natural pendulum path it had taken to go up.

Box Jumps

Select a steady box, bench or platform of a height comfortable for you. Stand facing it.

Jump off the floor on to the box/platform/bench.

Land softly (without making a loud noise when your feet touch the box) in a controlled motion, bang in the middle of the box.

You should land in a half squat position similar to this.

Stand up tall on the box before stepping down or jumping off it.

Side view: Select a steady box, bench or platform of a height comfortable for you. Stand facing it.

Side view: Jump off the floor on to the box/platform/bench.

Side view: You should land in a half squat position similar to this.

Side view: Stand up tall on the box before stepping down or jumping off it.

Step-ups

Select a steady box, bench or platform of a height comfortable for you. Stand facing it.

Like you climb stairs, raise one foot and plant it on the centre of the box/bench/platform.

Now, bring the second foot up on the box/bench/platform and stand straight on it.

Step off the box and back on to the floor, one foot at a time. All through the exercise, keep your core and gluteus muscles engaged.

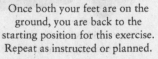

Once both your feet are on the ground, you are back to the starting position for this exercise. Repeat as instructed or planned.

Push-ups

Get into the plank position on your palms as shown in the picture. Make sure to engage your core all through the exercise for best results.

In a controlled motion, lower your chest and the rest of your body towards the floor.

Go down till your chest touches the floor. However, your hips remain off the floor and in a straight line with your back.

Side view: Get into the plank position on your palms as shown in the picture. Make sure to engage your core all through the exercise for best results.

Side view: In a controlled motion, lower your chest and the rest of your body towards the floor.

Side view: Go down till your chest touches the floor. However, your hips remain off the floor and in a straight line with your back.

Sit-ups

Lie flat on your back and fold your legs to form a diamond.
Put your hands behind your head on the floor.

Squeeze your abs and come up to a sitting position, with
your back straight and hands reaching up to the ceiling.
Go back flat on your back and touch the floor with your
hands behind your head. Come back up again.

Hollow Hold

Start by lying flat on your back. Lift your feet and arms about a feet off the floor while engaging your core muscles. Make sure your shoulder blades aren't in contact with the floor. Hold for 30 to 60 seconds.

V-ups

Lie flat on your back and lift your feet off the floor towards the ceiling.

Simultaneously, lift your arms and upper body off the floor till your hands touch the toes. From here, lower both your body and feet back to sleeping position and repeat the movement.

Plank

Lie flat on your stomach and then prop your body up on your toes and elbows such that your back is straight and the hips are in line with the spine, parallel to the floor. Make sure you engage your core and hips, your feet are together and you are looking straight ahead. Hold for 30 seconds at least.

Side Plank

Lie on the floor sideways. Now, lift your body sideways on your feet and one elbow. The other hand rests folded on your hips or is stretched out towards the ceiling. Core and hip muscles should be engaged. Hold for a minimum of 30 seconds. Repeat on the other side as well.

Mountain Climbers

Start by holding a plank on your palms. While keeping the core engaged, bring one leg forward such that the knee comes close to your chest.

Now, take the leg back to the starting position.

As soon as the first leg is back in starting position, move the other leg forward such that the knee is close to the chest. Perform these movements rapidly in quick succession.

Burpees

Crouch on the floor with your palms planted firmly on the floor about shoulder width apart.

Begin by standing straight on the floor.

Now, kick your legs back far enough for you to be able to straighten your body into a plank.

In a controlled manner, lower your body towards the floor into a push-up.

Go down till your chest is flat on the floor.

Push yourself back up into a plank.

Now, keeping your palms on the floor bring your legs forward with a slight jump such that you are back in the crouching position.

Get back on your feet and in the same motion jump about six inches off the floor, clapping your hands above your head. Land on the floor and bring your hands down.

Return to the starting position with your hands resting around your thighs. You are ready to go again.

Supine Pull-ups/Ring Rows/Reverse Pull-ups

Get a TRX band, Roman rings or a horizontal bar that comes up to your ribcage or chest. Grip the bar/rings/TRX band tightly and engage your core. Position your feet such that you can lean back and stretch your arms completely.

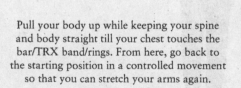

Pull your body up while keeping your spine and body straight till your chest touches the bar/TRX band/rings. From here, go back to the starting position in a controlled movement so that you can stretch your arms again.

Pull-ups

Find a bar high enough such that when you hang from it your feet do not touch the floor.

Now, engage your core and keeping your body as steady as possible, pull yourself up using the muscles in your back and arms.

Make sure you pull yourself up till the chin touches, or is level with, the bar that you are hanging from.

In a controlled motion, let yourself down till your
hands are fully stretched. Now you are ready to
start again.

Lunges

Stand straight with your feet together. Take a step forward and, if you want to make it more challenging, raise your hands over your head. Now, lower the back knee to the floor such that the front leg makes a 90-degree angle at the knee. Stand up and repeat with the other leg.

Side view: Stand straight with your feet together. Take a step forward and, if you want to make it more challenging, raise your hands over your head. Now, lower the back knee to the floor such that the front leg makes a 90-degree angle at the knee. Stand up and repeat with the other leg.

Foam Rolling and Warm-up

Place the foam roller on the floor and lie down with your lower back directly on it. Fold your legs and cross your arms such that each hand rests on the opposite shoulder. Your hips should touch the floor.

Raise your hips off the floor and move up and down to massage your back with the roller.

You could even extend your arms overhead to increase the pressure on the back and to stretch it.

Turn sideways and place your thigh directly on the foam roller while crossing your other leg over and placing the foot on the ground. Use your hands to balance yourself and then move up and down the foam roller to massage and mobilize your quadriceps. Repeat on the other leg too.

Stretching

5

Mind over Body

Have you watched Roger Federer play? Have you closely watched him in action? Next time, pay attention—to him or to any other world-class athlete or sportsman. Playing five punishing sets of tennis or sprinting 100 metres in just nine seconds are extremely draining physically. Equally difficult is watching your opponent double up in pain because of cramps or an injury.

Watch Federer. He lets his head rule both his musculoskeletal system and all feelings of sympathy. His ruthless focus doesn't waver, and his expression

---

Workout No. 8

Five rounds, 1 min each
Superman holds
Planks
Crunches
Leg raises

never changes till the match ends. After that, not only does he let a smile escape but also offers a warm handshake to his opponent with a query about the pain he went through during the game. The match is played out not just on the court, but also in Federer's mind.

And who hasn't seen that famous video of Usain Bolt grinning at Canada's Andre De Grasse in the 200-metre semi-final at the Rio Olympics in 2016? Before that broad smile, however, Bolt was serious, pushing just hard enough to stay ahead. His only aim was to finish first. Despite De Grasse's late charge, which one may suspect he knew was futile, Bolt was never threatened. He picked up just a little pace and finished ahead of the Canadian, both looking each other in the eye and grinning. After that they walked away in a mutual embrace, chatting with each other. Bolt later said that he was telling the Canadian that he made him run harder than he intended to. The jokes, however, began after the competition was over. The Canadian's performance ensured that Bolt was more vigilant. In fact, he was even more focused in the final, running the perfect race to clinch another Olympic gold without any trouble.

Fitness, like everything else, begins in the mind. Any athlete, world-class or otherwise, will agree with this without a second thought. When most people are given a workout, the first thing they tell their trainers is, 'This is difficult'. They start bargaining.

They talk the trainers into making concessions and relaxing the routine. If pull-ups are a problem, they will ask for these to be dropped altogether; if ten push-ups edge them slightly out of their comfort zone, they would settle for no more than six. And then, when they don't see results after three months, they ask the trainers, 'Why have I not made any progress . . . lost weight . . . built muscle?' In that moment of revelation, they refuse to entertain any attempt by the trainers to recap the hard bargain they drove each time they were given a workout. When you start a healthy lifestyle with this kind of mindset, you are unlikely to achieve the body or results you desire. That's because you are already defeated in your mind.

People who enrol for our Shivfit programmes are trained to prepare themselves mentally before they hit the floor and start working out. For some time now, I have been practising this myself before each session. This focus on exercising the mind has helped me immensely, not only in achieving fitness goals, but also in bringing sufficient clarity of thought to positively affect the way I approach life and the problems it throws at me. Not just has it helped me overcome personal problems, but also allowed me to cope better with injuries during my journey to fitness and emerge stronger.

I was once young and reckless, as most of us at that age usually are. It was fun to be that way.

Clearly, I was not smart enough to use my mind much except on how to impress women or pick up the best themes for parties. Having said that, I must mention that exercise was important to me even during that phase. I worked out regularly but without giving it too much thought. In our twenties, muscles build fast, heal quickly, and the body can take a lot. But after a point I had to grow up and change my ways. In 2010, at the age of twenty-seven, I was in the best shape of my life, my fitness was at its peak and I was on track to make it to the CrossFit Games finals in the United States of America. I was participating in the regionals and was ranked ninth in all of Asia. But CrossFit had not become as great a movement as it is today, and I was caught up with other things that life brings with it. Plus, there was the question of finding a sponsor, which is always difficult for a relatively little-known fitness competition. So, I decided not to go.

By the following year, CrossFit was a global movement and was fast becoming an unstoppable trend in India too. I started training again for the CrossFit Games, determined to sail through the regionals in Asia and make it to the finals in the USA. When the first workout was announced, I was quite pumped up and confident. I started out strong and performed well. But tragedy struck soon after. Just before the second workout was announced, a bus hit me while I was on my motorbike outside my gym in Juhu. It was 9.30 p.m. and I was headed to the gym to train. But instead of sweating it out, I lay doubled up on a busy Mumbai road with my bike scratched and dented. Although I was lucky enough to escape without a scratch and had sustained no external wounds, I had landed awkwardly, which led to my shoulders and back taking the impact of the crash. When I returned to the gym a few days later, I started by warming-up. When I got into position to do a few push-ups, I found myself in tremendous pain. It was so bad that I couldn't manage a single push-up.

Scans revealed soft tissue damage. The injury was more serious than I had imagined it to be. I was disappointed and dejected at not being able to compete in the CrossFit Games, but it was nothing compared to what lay in store for me. For the next nine months, I couldn't do a single push-up. Every time I tried, excruciating pain reminded me that restlessness would not take me anywhere. I felt frustrated, and it was as if the universe was conspiring against me. Fortunately, my friend, celebrity trainer and Shivfit co-founder, Vrinda Mehta, was at hand. She sensed my troubles. It was she who made me realize the importance of mental conditioning and a positive frame of mind. With her help, I started meditating. She showed me how to channel my internal energy and thoughts, and use the limitless energy of the sun to improve myself. During those months, not only did I recuperate, I also became more and more aware of myself and the power of my mind. Slowly, one small step at a time, as she helped me through the recovery process, I started discovering how important a role our mind plays in everything we do—from maths to lifting weights to Sudoku to our constant search for success. As I learnt how to meditate better, I found myself to be a lot more positive in everything I did. Bad news or a plan gone wrong did not anger or disappoint me any longer. People, traffic and all the other things that had been frequent sources of irritation didn't bother me so much any more. Meditation helped me tide over a very frustrating and difficult period in my life and made me stronger to face the challenges ahead. And there were plenty of them.

The advantages of positive thinking are backed by a fair bit of research. In early 2017, a paper in the *American Journal of Epidemiology*, which was based on an eight-year-long study involving over 70,000 women, found that optimists were less likely to die from cancer, heart diseases, strokes, lung conditions or infections than pessimists. 'Optimism doesn't set people up for disappointment—studies show it provides resilience against distress. In people with head and neck cancer, the more optimistic reported a better quality of life regardless of the stage of the condition,' British newspaper *Guardian* reported while discussing the landmark study.

'The research finds that optimists don't just expect good things to happen, they actively take steps to make them happen. They lead healthier lives because they believe it will benefit them. It is hypothesized, without much evidence, that optimists feel less negativity and so produce fewer bursts of stress-related hormones such as cortisol and adrenaline, which can increase blood pressure.'[1] Given the benefits of training one's mind, I sometimes regret not starting out earlier.

There are several techniques of meditation. The one that helped me personally, and which I still practise, is Surya Yog, which teaches you to channel the sun's energy through your mind and body. I also practise breathing exercises, which can help you breathe better during workouts, thus allowing you to keep at it for longer.

But I was yet to understand what an important role learning to put the mind over matter was to play in my life. It didn't take too long. In 2012, just as

[1] Luisa Dillner, 'Can Optimism Make You Live Longer, *The Guardian*, 6 March 2017, https://www. theguardian.com/lifeandstyle/2017/mar/06/can-optimism-make-you-live-longer

the CrossFit Games were closing in, I was forced to
summon all my positivity and mental strength once
again. After the accident, it took me nine months
to get back to prime fitness and go back to doing
push-ups. Through those months, I remained patient
and adapted my workouts in a way that helped
me maintain decent fitness levels without doing
the exercises that I was unable to do. Though the
recovery was slow, I could feel myself getting better
every day. Slowly and surely, I emerged stronger.
Once again, the CrossFit Games were beckoning. In
the weeks leading up to the announcement of the
competition, I had been putting in long hours in
the box, working out up to three times a day. But
one evening, when I was stretching, my hamstring
gave way. I was in tremendous pain and couldn't
move. The other people in the gym had to pick me
up, put me in a vehicle and drive me home. It was
worse than when I had met with the accident. But
since the discomfort wasn't intense the next day,
I dismissed it, assuming it to be a result of intense
training. In fact, my hamstrings hurt so much that it
would take me ten minutes to just wear my shorts.
I was forced to undergo an MRI test to determine
what exactly was wrong. It turned out to be calcified
tendonitis, which occurs when an injury continues
to happen over a long period of time and your body
starts depositing calcium over the tendons to make

them harder in an attempt to keep the muscle from tearing. Apparently, the injury from the accident hadn't healed completely, and whenever I pushed myself it would relapse. Over time, the body did its job and left me in extreme pain. I can only blame bad luck that seemed to have followed me stubbornly as far as the CrossFit Games were concerned. I never managed to make it to the event as an athlete. Each time I tried, I ended up injured. Finally, in 2015, I decided to go for the finals as a spectator. I was fit as a fiddle and got a chance to work out with several CrossFit legends such as Jason Khalipa, Samantha Briggs and Chris Spealler in gyms across the USA. Sometimes that is how life works. The younger me would have been furious at this rather cruel joke, but the post-meditation, wiser me was content and appreciated the positive side of such an opportunity.

This significant change in attitude and training—where I started applying my mind and was more positive—had a direct impact on my physical prowess as well. Now that I didn't bring stress, anxiety and anger into my exercise regimen, I was seeing better results and performing more efficiently.

It is impossible to ensure that all members of your gym are happy always. Like most other people, some of my clients may be having trouble in their relationships, at work, or in their businesses. Except a few, most of them can't let go of their problems—

even for an hour—for their fitness targets. They may ace the workout despite the stress and anxiety, but they struggle to see the results that their efforts should have otherwise yielded. Funnily enough, our body is a slave to the mind, and if the mind isn't fit, physical fitness is most likely to remain elusive. Do you think you can call yourself fit if you run a marathon, get in five decent workouts a week, or squat thrice your body weight but cannot get through the day without a panic attack triggered by stress or can't sleep properly at night? When you are in such a state of mind, you cannot do strenuous physical activity for too long. You are fit only when your mind and body both are healthy—what you might hear people on television market as holistic fitness.

After the accident outside the gym, the other technique that I learnt and practised throughout my recovery period, apart from meditation, was visualization. All top sportsmen practise this. That's how they are able to anticipate their rival's next moves and also plan strategies that help them win.

Workout No. 9

Three to five rounds
25 sit-ups
1-min plank
25 hollow rocks
1-min hollow hold

The best thing about visualization, which I discovered over time, is that it comes in handy in all situations. It can, in fact, prepare you for challenges ahead, besides helping you on your way to success. Again, I have to thank Vrinda for this. She has trained the royalty of Bollywood, including the Bachchans, and taught them how to use this technique expertly to their own advantage. It may sound complex, but it is a very simple exercise.

All you need to do is have an image of your goal in mind. Then chart your path from your current situation till your goal in several progressive stages, with images for each. For example, if your goal is having six-pack abs, and at present you are slightly overweight with a fair layer of fat around the midriff, this is how you need to do it: first, pick your goal. If you like, use photoshop to morph a picture of yourself and airbrush it as close to your target as possible. Put it up on a board where you can see it clearly.

Next, break that goal up into smaller targets and prepare images for each. So, the first stage would be gradual fat loss, especially around the midriff. For this, you can come up with a morphed image of yourself about five to ten kilograms lighter, with less fat around the midriff. Keep going till you plan ten stages—from the start till the end—all accompanied by images. Now that you know what you are targeting, it is easier to plan a programme and stick to it. Whenever you feel you have made some progress, click a selfie on your smartphone, print it and compare it to the ten images to see which one it resembles the most. Stick it next to that image and put down the date, weight and waistline. This way you will have a timeline of your progress and will be able to track it actively till you reach your goal. In real life, too, once you identify the objective, you can set smaller targets that lead up to it.

However, there are a few things that you need to be careful about while using the visualization method. If you set unreal targets, you are bound to fail and end up dejected. So, keep your goals practical, thus ensuring that you neither set an extremely easy goal, nor an absolutely unrealistic one. All you need to do is push just a little beyond your comfort zone.

Another crucial thing is *time*. Do not go about setting impossible timelines. More often than not, shortcuts in life are fraught with danger and risks. In fitness, shortcuts can cause serious injuries. Have patience and set reasonable time targets. On the flipside, don't be so lazy that you take six months for a goal that can be achieved in just two. Be alert and stay focused.

Also, be diligent. Quitters are not successful. Even if progress is slow, stick to your plan and tick off one mini goal after another. You might get bored at times. There will also be instances when you feel like you aren't making any headway, but if all other factors are optimal and you stay on track with your plan, you are actually making progress.

Finally, the last step to achieving the goal is usually the most difficult. It is quite like the final assault on the summit of a mountain. Not only is the final ascent going to be a tad bit more difficult than the rest of the journey, but it will be even more troublesome thanks to the nervous energy and restlessness you are likely to experience as the goal inches closer. For example, you are likely to lose most of your belly fat with regular exercise and proper nutrition in a few months, but the last bit of the belly roll, famously and correctly called *stubborn fat*, might take almost the same amount of time to disappear and unveil the six-pack abs you have been working so hard for.

6

Nutrition: You Are What You Eat

Ultimately, it all comes down to what you eat. And drink.

You could be a dedicated gym buff who follows all the exercise routines to a T and yet, chances are, you might not see the results that you had expected—unless, of course, you paid attention to your diet and nutrition. There is a difference between the two, which will be discussed later in the chapter. For now, let us concentrate on understanding how and why food intake can affect the results of your exercise.

If you have ever heard the claim that 'fitness is just 30 per cent physical exercise and 70 per cent diet', don't dismiss it without a thought. The person you heard it from may not know exactly how or why that statement works, but he or she is definitely not wrong. You are what you eat, much more than what you exercise.

Generally speaking, you will be a healthy individual if you pay attention to what you consume—every meal, every day. It means you have to be extremely disciplined about what, how much and when you eat. It is rare to come across people like that, simply because it is human to err. All of us give in to temptation once in a while: that piece of dark chocolate, the comfort of an ice cream on a bright sunny day, that extra cup of coffee or tea, and that one last drink. How many friends, friends of friends, family members or colleagues do you know who can say 'no' to crunchy French fries or a delicate dessert? Add to that the fact that most ready-to-eat products in the market, even the so-called healthy ones, contain sugar, which research has shown to be our biggest enemy. So, to make up for our eating and drinking digressions, we have to work out both to stay in shape and to remain healthy.

When we work out, our body burns carbohydrates and fat, which are the fuel we function on. They are stored in our bodies and come from the food we eat.

Our muscles, which undergo a lot of wear and tear during physical exercise, use the protein we eat to repair themselves, as well as aid recovery and counter muscle fatigue. Proper protein intake helps beat delayed onset of muscle soreness (DOMS), besides building more muscle. More often than not, if we don't follow a particular diet, whether it is under guidance or our own design, we end up eating more or less fat than we burn. We all know what happens when we eat more fat than what we burn: we put on flab and get tyres and muffin tops. However, when our carb and fat intake is lower than what is needed, we enter a dangerous phase that should be avoided at all costs. When that happens, we start losing muscle mass, which means we start losing volume, definition and (a lot of) weight too. Because muscle is heavier than fat, when we start burning it the weighing scale starts showing drastic results. Losing weight through muscle loss is not healthy and should be avoided. Hence, having a diet fine-tuned to your level of physical activity is very important. That is where nutritionists and dieticians come in.

Earlier, I had mentioned that nutrition and diet sound the same but are two very different things. Without delving too deep into technical details and science, let us get a simplistic understanding of what the two terms broadly mean. Diet is what we consume (both eat and drink) through the day, while nutrition is the nutrients such as carbohydrates, proteins, fat and minerals our body absorbs from the food and drinks we consume.

The Merriam Webster online dictionary defines nutrition as, 'the act or process of nourishing or being nourished'. Hence, a dietician will focus on what you eat and how much, while the nutritionist will be concerned with how much and which nutrients your body gets from your diet. A simple example can illustrate the difference. When you pick up an energy bar, the ingredients listed are of interest to the dietician, while the percentage of protein, carbohydrates, fats, etc. is what will matter to the nutritionist.

Now that you have some understanding of the two terms, let us get a little more technical about how diet and exercise work in tandem. Your diet directly affects your exercise. How much you exercise dictates how much you eat post-workout and pre-workout. Both meals play very different roles. While a post-workout meal aids recovery, building of muscles, refuelling and rehydrating the body, a pre-workout meal improves performance, sustains energy, maintains and protects muscle mass and hydrates the body. The pre-workout meal should be consumed at least an hour before exercising, while the post-workout meal is best eaten within twenty

---

Workout No. 10

Five rounds
4 mins AMRAP, 1 min rest between each
3 burpees
6 push-ups
9 squats

minutes of completing the routine for best results. More often than not, we also need some sort of drinks during exercise. The intra-workout meal's aim is to keep the body hydrated, provide immediate fuel and preserve muscles.

You also need to eat and drink on your rest days when you aren't working out. Now, those meals play a different role. Since so much of our time is spent eating and drinking (our regular meals, snacks, coffee, tea, aerated drinks, alcoholic beverages, finger food at the bar and so on), let's turn our focus to what you usually want to gloss over as quickly as possible or avoid talking about: what you ought to eat.

An average person ends up eating much more than what his or her body needs—quite the opposite of what truly fit athletes do in their prime and even afterwards. Add to that the social pressure of having a 'good time', which usually means consuming alcoholic or sugary beverages about once a week on an average. Also, the fact that there is so much printed material—in newspapers, magazines and on websites—on what constitutes a healthy diet, that it becomes confusing for a person to decide what and how one should eat. When confronted with such a dilemma, it is best to ignore all advice. That's exactly what I do. It is better to turn to more informed sources, such as your trainer or coach, depending on how much confidence you have in him or her, or a nutritionist. But if you don't want to go to these lifestyle experts, the best thing to do would be to try various diets and their combinations and list what works for you and what doesn't. Through trial and error you will come up with a food plan that is ideal for you. It takes time, but the results are better. Later in this chapter, I'll outline how you can do that.

Before we start discussing the more fashionable and scientific diets, let us see what government bodies have laid down in their diet and nutrition guidelines. The National Institute of Nutrition, India last updated its guidelines, *Dietary Guidelines for Indians—A Manual,* in 2011, which talks about the importance of a balanced diet and exercise.[1]

Its guidelines state:

- *Nutrition is a basic prerequisite to sustain life.*
- *Variety in food is not only the spice of life but also the essence of nutrition and health.*
- *A diet consisting of foods from several food groups provides all the required nutrients in proper amounts.*

---

[1] National Institute of Nutrition, Indian Council of Medical Research, *Dietary Guidelines For Indians—A Manual.* (2011 ICMR, Hyderabad, India), second edition, p. 11, http://ninindia.org/dietaryguidelinesforninwebsite.pdf

– Cereals, millets and pulses are major sources of most nutrients.

– Milk, which provides good quality proteins and calcium, must be an essential item of the diet, particularly for infants, children and women.

– Oils and nuts are calorie-rich foods, and are useful for increasing the energy density and quality of food.

– Inclusion of eggs, flesh foods and fish enhances the quality of diet. However, vegetarians can derive almost all the nutrients from cereals, pulses, vegetables, fruits and milk-based diets.

– Vegetables and fruits provide protective substances such as vitamins, minerals, phytonutrients.

– Diversified diets with a judicious choice from a variety of food groups provide the necessary nutrients.

The National Institute of Nutrition has also drawn up a food pyramid with things that we ought to consume adequately right at the bottom, things to eat liberally above it, things to eat moderately above that and what to eat sparingly right on top. Below the pyramid are two signs advising you to *abstain from alcohol* and *say no to tobacco*. Alongside the pyramid is a colourful blurb exclaiming in bold, 'Exercise regularly and be physically active'.

The text-heavy 127-page document with blurry images in graphics and multiple text-heavy, jargon filled tables also defines what a balanced diet for Indians is.

'A balanced diet is one which provides all nutrients in required amounts and proper proportions. It can easily be achieved through a blend of the four basic food groups. The quantity of foods needed to meet nutrient requirements vary with age, gender, physiological status and physical activity. A balanced diet should provide around 50 to 60 per cent of total calories from carbohydrates, preferably from complex carbohydrates, about 10 to 15 per cent from proteins and 20 to 30 per cent from both visible and invisible fat.

In addition, a balanced diet should provide other non-nutrients such as dietary fibre, antioxidants and phytochemicals, which bestow positive health benefits. Antioxidants such as vitamins C and E, beta-carotene, riboflavin and selenium protect the body from free radical damage. Other phytochemicals such as polyphenols, flavones, etc. also afford protection against oxidant damage. Spices like turmeric, ginger, garlic, cumin and cloves are rich in antioxidants.'

This isn't the most comprehensive advice and won't help you plan your diet to the last morsel, but it does lay down the basic tenets of a healthy diet in its recommendation of '50 to 60 per cent of total calories from carbohydrates, preferably from complex carbohydrates, about 10 to 15 per cent from proteins and 20 to 30 per cent from both visible and invisible fat'. Since it's tough to ascertain the percentage of each type of food in our meals, this may not be the most practical advice, but it does provide basic guidelines.

Since we take cues on lifestyle, health and fitness from the West, and also because we visibly see the difference between their general fitness and our own levels of fitness, let us take a look at what Britain and the United States' nutrition and health authorities have laid down in their guidelines for a balanced, healthy diet.

For a regular, active individual, Britain's National Health Service (NHS) suggests the Eatwell Plate plan. With a picture of a plate, representing a pie chart, the Eatwell Plate tells you how much to eat from which food group. Each portion of the pie chart is colour-coded and includes pictures of foods that ought to be consumed. It also says that for a healthy normal adult male, the consumption, including all foods and drinks, should be 2500 calories each day, while that for a female should be 2000 calories. 'The Eatwell Guide shows how much of what we eat overall should come from which food group to achieve a healthy, balanced diet. You don't need to achieve this balance with every meal but try to get the balance right over a day or even a week,'[2] the NHS says on its website.

Fruits and vegetables make up a big chunk of the plate. The guidelines under the visual representation instruct one to eat at least five portions of fruits and vegetables every day. They should make up over a third of what one eats daily.

An equal portion of the Eatwell Plate is made up of carbohydrates such as potatoes, bread, rice, pasta and other starchy carbs. 'Starchy food should make up just over a third of the food we eat. Choose higher-fibre, wholegrain varieties, such as wholewheat pasta and brown rice, or simply leave the potato skins on. There are also higher-fibre versions of white bread and pasta. Starchy foods are a good source of energy and the main source of a range of nutrients in our diet,' the NHS instructs.

A significantly smaller portion of the plate contains images of beans, pulses, fish, eggs, meat and other sources of proteins. These have to be consumed in smaller quantities. 'Aim for at least two portions of fish every week—one of which should be oily, such as salmon or mackerel,' the NHS says.

An even smaller segment of the plate is filled up with dairy products and alternatives such as soya

---

2 National Health Service, http://www.nhs.uk/Livewell/ Goodfood/Pages/the-eatwell-guide.aspx

drinks and yoghurt. Milk, cheese and yoghurt are a great source of protein, calcium and even some vitamins. The plan, however, asks people to stick to low-fat and low-fat options of dairy products.

A small sliver of the Eatwell Plate pie chart indicates the food that we ought to eat the least. This group contains unsaturated fats such as olive, rapeseed, sunflower and vegetable oils as well as low-fat butter and spreads. Since all types of fats are high on energy, these should be consumed in small amounts only.

The plan puts foods high in fat, salt and sugar, such as chocolates, cakes, biscuits, ghee, butter, ice creams and carbonated drinks outside the plate. These, according to the guidelines, should be consumed less often and in small amounts only as they are not needed in one's diet.

The plan also advises that one ought to drink as much as six to eight glasses of fluids, including water, tea, coffee and beverages that are low on sugar each day. 'Fruit juice and smoothies also count towards your fluid consumption but they contain free sugars that can damage the teeth, so limit these to a combined total of 150 millilitres per day,' the NHS says.

The Brits are also told that they do not need to strike this balance for every meal or even in the course of one day. That isn't humanly possible.

They need to achieve this balance on a weekly and monthly basis. This allows for a cheat day as long as one averages it out with disciplined eating days and meals.

As we see, both dietary guidelines—Indian and British—pretty much say the same thing, varying slightly in the details. It is the ease of use and simple language that makes the British plan more useful.

The Fashion Diets

Like all things government, few take note of the official dietary advice issued by it. Those who do take a look do not take it too seriously. This is where the fancy celebrity-endorsed diets come in. Backed by just about enough scientific data to back their claims, these trendy diets are marketed cleverly by well-toned, impeccably-shaped celebrity faces swearing by them. Soon enough, they become successful as thousands of gullible people follow in the celebrities' footsteps in search of that elusive ideal physique. Remember what a rage the Atkins Diet used to be in the early '90s? After 2012, Paleo, Alkaline, 5:2, 80:20 and Sugar Detox became a rage but were later pushed out of the collective awareness by something newer. As of 2017, the diets that are making waves are DASH, MIND and Mediterranean.

Meanwhile, Paleo continues to be popular, thanks to the surging demand for CrossFit among the masses. Boycotting all forms of sugar is still fashionable and believed to be good for health, with no small thanks to the efforts of author and researcher Robert Lustig and his battle against refined sugar. Even the good old Atkins Diet seems to have got a new lease of life. Let's try and understand these fashion diets better.

Paleo Diet: It's time to go back to eating like the caveman—that's the central premise of this diet. The proponents of the Paleo diet contend that our ancestors were fitter than us. So, what they ate back then is what we should eat today. This diet requires you to eat food that can be hunted, fished and gathered such as natural proteins (meat, fish, vegetables, fruits) and healthy fats (nuts, meat, etc.). It requires you to shun modern-day processed foods, legumes, grains, dairy, pulses and sugar. The focus of this regimen is on eating a good variety of foods with special attention to fruits, vegetables and good carbs.

An abundance of protein-rich foods means this diet, when properly complemented with exercise, shows you the promise of lean muscle gain, weight loss and more vitality. As part of this diet, the intake of compounds related to inflammation and acidity is much lower. It includes foods that don't raise insulin levels and ensures a healthy intake of fibre since it is a produce-based diet. However, one is restricted to a limited choice of food items while adhering to this plan.

The good news is that you can eat all Indian vegetable and meat preparations cooked with less spice and salt. You are allowed to use ghee and/or coconut oil for all cooking. Any homemade chicken recipe made with milder spices and Paleo-friendly oils, fresh fruits and vegetables, nuts and seeds can also feature in your diet. However, you will have to avoid all legumes, grains, refined oils, extra spices, salt and dairy products.

But, be careful. Like almost everything on this planet, the Paleo diet has its drawbacks. Not only is modern man not the same as his ancestors, most fruits and vegetables available today are not what they used to be back in the caveman days. Most modern meats aren't the same either. So, this diet could lead

---

Workout No. 11

Five rounds, 1 min each
Complete the following reps in one minute:
7 burpees
10 push-ups
12 sit-ups
15 squats
The faster you finish the reps the more rest you get

to nutrient deficiency. The benefits of legumes far outweigh their anti-nutrient content. Legumes also have great antioxidants and anti-cancer properties that you may be deprived of. Also, no dairy food could cause bone problems. Additionally, people with special health conditions and food restrictions cannot follow this, while for vegetarians and vegans, this is a very difficult diet to adopt and adapt to.

The 5:2 Diet: Based on the principle of intermittent fasting, this diet lets you eat normally five days a week, while for two non-consecutive days you need to restrict your consumption to 600 calories per day for men and 500 calories per day for women. Fasting is never done on two consecutive days. In dietary terms, normal means controlled and clean eating. Because of its roots in intermittent fasting, this diet helps lose weight, helps keep blood pressure and cholesterol levels within the healthy range and leads to an increase in life span.

The upside, apart from the health benefits, of the 5:2 diet is that it gives one the mental satiety of eating a wide range of foods with no restriction for five out of seven days and yet shows results. However, two days of restricted eating (600 calories or less) can lead to severe nutrient deficiency. There is also the risk that fasting could induce overeating the following day. Fasting is also known to lead to anxiety and sleep deprivation. Additionally, this plan could result in great fluctuations in weight once discontinued.

On fasting days, you could plan meals that include egg and toast for breakfast, fruits and milk, followed by grilled or steamed chicken/fish with sauté vegetables and brown rice for the other meals. Vegetarians can plan porridge/oats/poha/idli with fruits and milk, followed by sauté vegetables with brown rice/vegetable biryani. On the other five days, normal healthy eating is recommended.

The 80:20 Diet: More than a diet, this is a lifestyle change, considering it requires you to ensure that 80 per cent of your meals are clean and the remaining 20 per cent can be an indulgence, a treat for the discipline you have shown earlier. This plan is more sustainable than other fashionable diets because it is not very rigid. It also allows you to enjoy the occasional cocktail and dessert while keeping your weight in check. It works on the principle that better food habits and a healthier lifestyle will lead to better weight control and a healthy body.

This diet teaches healthy eating habits and makes one more aware of one's health. It also keeps weight, cholesterol and blood sugar levels in the desired range due to balanced eating patterns. The dark side, however, is that people tend to overexploit the 20 per cent freedom option and indulge in too much junk food.

During the clean eating period you can eat anything in moderation as long as it's healthy and not fried. Overeating is also a strict no-no. The rest of the time, even junk food is allowed occasionally. Go on and order that pizza, butter steak, cheesecake and beer, but in moderation.

Sugar Detox: Over the last couple of years, there has been a growing consensus among the health, fitness, medical and nutrition communities that sugar is the new enemy. Needless to say, this diet is trending currently. There is a range of sugar-free diets: some are extremely strict and forbid intake of sugar in all forms, while others focus on certain types of sugars. The strict ones forbid some dairy products, several fruits and even certain vegetables. But most of these focus on processed and refined sugar. So, forget those cakes, biscuits, sweet drinks and processed foods like cereals, bread and tomato ketchup. Fans of this diet cite weight loss, better immunity and more energy as results.

By removing sugar from your diet you end up eating less, avoid energy crashes, see weight loss, maintain healthy blood sugar levels and keep diabetes under control.

The sugar detox diet is easy to follow as long as you look out for the hidden sugars in processed and packaged foods. It also does not set any limit on portion sizes or ask you to maintain a calorie count, which can be detrimental if you tend to overeat. The best part about this is that it omits bad carbs and hence is good for weight loss and checking diabetes.

The extreme versions of this diet exclude most fruits, which would result in important vitamins, antioxidants and phytochemicals not being available to you without supplements.

If you want to go on a sugar detox, you will need to start buying grass-fed meats, eggs, fish, nuts, vegetables, lentils, ghee, olive oil, coconut oil, butter, lemons and wholegrains like wheat, brown rice, bajra, etc. And while you are at it, also bid goodbye to alcohol, MSG and simple carbs—white pasta, white rice and white bread. You can't have any simple sugars, artificial sweeteners, fruits and fruit juices either.

Alkaline: Gwyneth Paltrow, Victoria Beckham and Jennifer Aniston were the star followers of this diet. If that's not reason enough for you to give this a try, let the scientific principle it is based on make an attempt. Excess acid in your body is converted into fat. High acidity levels also cause a number of other problems like heartburn, gastric problems, and kidney and liver disorders. Now, who wants to gain fat or live with a bum liver and kidney?

The alkaline diet recommends cutting back on meat, wheat, other grains, refined sugar, dairy products, caffeine, alcohol and processed foods. These are to be replaced with alkaline foods such as fruits and vegetables, which reduce the body's acidity levels. The basic premise is that an alkaline diet helps maintain healthy acidity levels.

Consuming more food that is metabolized into alkaline residues and lesser of what is metabolized into acidic residues can help preserve muscle mass. Supporters of this diet also claim that it makes you look younger since it avoids refined sugar and helps you cut down on calories and weight. If you are a vegan, this a great diet to turn to.

Most herbs and spices such as ginger, garlic, black and white pepper, cumin, mustard, fennel, clove and cardamom, are alkaline-forming. So, this must come as music to those who love Indian food. Also, stock your refrigerators with fruits and dry fruits including almonds, raisins, dates, apricots, mangoes, guavas, lychees, peaches, coconuts, lemons and limes and vegetables such as eggplant, zucchini, tomatoes, potato skin, mushrooms, peas, carrots, broccoli, cauliflower, spinach, and green beans. You can also have ghee and lentils. Be ready to say goodbye to salt, rice, lamb, bread, chicken, fish, dried beans, cashews, peanuts, pistachios, cottage cheese and yoghurt. Fruits, including berries and plums, canned juices, and vegetables such as beans and cooked spinach are also a no-no.

But be warned, our bodies like acids just as much as they like the alkalis. During the early days of this diet, the body is likely to witness a shift in pH balance as it is not designed for such an eating pattern. At times, this diet can get very confusing. For example, lemons and apple cider, which are acidic in nature, are listed as alkaline because of the way they are metabolized by the body.

DASH (Dietary Approaches to Stop Hypertension): As the name suggests, DASH is an eating plan that is preventive and precautionary in nature. In this approach, foods are selected carefully with the aim of preventing, as well as lowering, high blood pressure and hypertension. In January 2017, it was considered the best overall diet in the US according to a handful of polls and surveys.

One of the reasons this is such a big hit is because it allows for a lot of flexibility and gives people the option of not having to track everything they eat as long as they consume enough fruits, vegetables, wholegrains, lean proteins and low-fat dairy products while staying away from fried, fat and calorie-rich foods and red meats. However, people need to consciously lower their intake of salt.

Mediterranean Diet: This diet made a splash in the US all through 2016 and the beginning of 2017. One of the biggest reasons for this is that the Mediterranean diet lets people eat most of the things they grow up on—of course not junk food—and also allows for the occasional drink. It places foods in a pyramid structure, with those than one must eat right at the bottom and those that should be eaten in minimum quantities on the top. Those who follow this diet need to include a lot of seasonal fresh fruits, vegetables, wholegrains, legumes, nuts and seeds in their daily intake. Fish and seafood can be consumed twice a week, with tuna, salmon, trout and mackerel being the healthy options. Cheese, yoghurt and other dairy products can be consumed at will as long as they are the low-fat or fat-free versions. One of the most important aspects of this diet is replacing the harmful fats—saturated and trans-fats—such as butter, margarine and oil with healthier fats such as olive oil and canola oil. The use of salt is also significantly reduced while herbs and spices are introduced. When it comes to red meat, this diet recommends replacing it with fish or poultry, with consumption limited to just a few times a month. Those following this diet must ensure that the meat is lean and doesn't contain too much fat. Consequently, bacon and sausages are to be avoided.

Like most other fashion diets discussed here, the aim of this diet is to ensure that the food you eat lowers your risk of heart disease and helps you avoid weight gain.

Do Diets Work?

All diet plans mentioned here, and for that matter most diets we hear about, focus on preventing diseases, weight management or having a healthy heart. None, with the exception of the Paleo diet, puts the onus on foods that boost fitness or athletic performance. So, if your focus is on building muscle and get fitter, none of these diets are right for you. A CrossFitter might swear by the Paleo diet but that doesn't necessarily mean it will work just as well for you. What works for you will depend on what your fitness goals are. For instance, if you want to be an endurance athlete and spend long hours doing the same activity or exercise, you will have to design a diet high in carbohydrates for yourself to be able to power through the long runs, bike rides and swims. However, if you want the lean muscular look, you will need to lift heavy weights and cut down your carb intake while increasing the amount of protein you consume every day.

A lot of film stars and sportspersons have dedicated teams with nutritionists and dieticians at their beck and call. Since their bodies are not only their temples but also the reason that they keep their jobs, they can afford to dedicate both time and money to such extravagances. Who hasn't heard of tennis star Novak Djokovic's fussiness when it comes to food? He loved pizzas, but after a nutritionist diagnosed that tomato, cheese and gluten were hampering his physical prowess he cut down on all three. Shortly after that he was in prime form physically and went on to rise to the number one spot. In fact, he has gone on record to say that he is so particular about his food that he cooks all meals himself even during tours.

Now, most of us are caught up in our daily lives with jobs, families and social commitments. That you manage to take out time for exercise is commendable in itself, so asking you to eke out some more time to cook the perfect meal is probably flirting with danger. Most of us do not have that kind of time at our disposal and our resources, too, would be stretched thin if we were to try and follow celebrity lifestyles. As a fitness trainer, I come across several nutritionists and dieticians, and each one has great ideas and advice. I listen to them all. I even experiment and follow every bit of new advice I get. Frankly, new ideas excite me and I like to put them to test. Needless to say, I have tried several diets and nutrition plans over the years and have seen a fair amount of success with some of them.

Through all this trial and error, I have realized that there is no tailor-made diet for any of us— we need to figure out what works best for us and stick to it. From time to time, our bodies undergo physiological changes, which might mean that what used to work for us for the longest time won't suit us any more and we may need to tweak our diet once again. Similar changes might be necessary when we experience emotional and psychological changes as well. From my experience with nutrition and diet, I can tell you that whenever I realized I was not getting the same results from my workouts, I experimented with my eating patterns, introduced items and discarded things I used to eat earlier. It was through trial and error that I identified the changes I needed to make to my diet to make it work.

To put it simply, my advice would be that you design your own diet based on the principles of what

---

Workout No. 12

Three to five rounds (45 seconds work, 15 seconds rest)
R-side plank
Plank
L-side plank
Hollow hold

a wholesome diet should be and after trying out a few combinations. Make note of everything that works for you and buy more of it. Throw out everything that doesn't work. Also, don't be too strict on yourself about eating clean every time you sit down for a meal. If you have been putting in quality time at the gym or you have been training, go and treat yourself to restricted food that you like once every fortnight. There is no harm in doing that as long as you do not binge on unhealthy stuff. Even the occasional drink is all right. We are, after all, humans and deserve to have some fun. I am a good Bombayite and hence do relish my occasional vada-pav and bhelpuri.

The Protein Shake Conundrum: To Have or Not to Have

Finally, let us turn to the protein supplement conundrum, which includes the classic protein shake and the new favourite—protein bars. Every time I meet a fresher in the gym, one of the first things they ask me is if they should start taking protein supplements? So, let me answer this one before you ask.

I know and have heard about several world-class athletes who are vegan and only depend on natural sources of protein that they get from their regular diets. You won't find them clasping a jar in one hand and shaking it vigorously to dissolve protein in water after every training session. They are famous for not taking protein supplements. At the other end of the spectrum are those who religiously take supplements before, during and after every workout. Most of us fall in between: serious enough to buy the recommended protein powder but relaxed enough to not fret over it if we forget to have it once in a while after a workout. Given how much these supplements cost, it is not a bad idea to forget them once in a while! Fitness, after and above all, ought to be affordable and not a burden.

The reason we need proteins is because it helps build muscles. Apart from that, proteins also aid recovery after the wear and tear we put them through while training. However, if you are among those who eats well and goes to the gym only two to three times a week, you are receiving enough protein from your regular diet through eggs, paneer, soya, yoghurt, meat, nuts, etc. Nutrition and health researchers have carried out studies and found evidence that those who work out twice a week on an average do not need to turn to protein supplements.[3] However,

---

[3] Haroon Siddique, 'Protein Hype: Shoppers Flushing Money Down The Toilet, Say Expert', *The Guardian*, 26 December 2016, https://www.theguardian.com/lifeandstyle/2016/dec/26/protein-hype-shoppers-flushing-money-down-the-toilet-say-experts

anyone who has ever been to a gym and consulted trainers will have heard the contrary.

Not surprisingly, there is evidence to show that the sales of protein shakes and bars have skyrocketed in recent times and that there is plenty to choose from. Brands that traditionally made chocolate and chocolate-based snacks, such as Mars and Snickers, have their own range of protein bars to offer. Among the general public, a greater number of people have become more conscious of what they put into their bodies. They choose protein over carbohydrates driven by the misplaced belief that less carbohydrates mean less fat and hence less weight. The United States Institute of Medicine stipulates a minimum of 0.8 gram of protein for every kg of body weight per day. Public Health England's guidelines recommend a protein intake of 55.5 grams for men and 45 grams for women aged between nineteen and sixty-four years.

Nutritionists, though not the ones employed at your gym, firmly believe that people who put in a mere two or three days at the gym do not require any protein supplements as they get enough from the food they consume. But these same people agree that athletes and those who train at high intensities for long hours each day do require the extra protein from supplements. Coming back to us, since protein supplements play an important psychological role by making us believe that we are making an improvement, it is just as well that we continue to take it. The good news is that we are doing the economy a favour and at the same time doing no harm to ourselves because the body excretes all the extra protein in our urine. But anyone with any condition related to the kidneys ought to be careful because the extra protein can have serious medical repercussions for them. Also, do not use protein shakes and bars as replacements for meals. Doing so only puts you at risk of doing more harm than good. The body loves its natural foods, such as fruits, vegetables and wholegrains.

Personally, I use protein shakes as often as possible. However, it does not mean the end of the world for me if I don't take it after every workout. Considering that I often workout twice or thrice a day at pretty high intensities, I do require the extra protein that I do not get from my diet. If you fall into this bracket as well, I suggest you do the same.

Workout Directory

This section outlines daily workouts, starting at the beginner's level and progressing to advanced ones. The empty columns are to help you track your fitness journey and improvement as you record the number of repetitions, rounds, time taken and weights used for each workout.

Be careful and don't overexert while doing the workouts. If something seems too tough, skip it. Everyone progresses differently and is better at certain exercises, so don't be disheartened if your first attempt isn't the best.

Some of the workouts mention two weights, separated by a /. The first number is the recommended weight for men while the second figure is the recommended weight for women. Pick according to your comfort level. Progress to weights only once you are confident (see Chapter 3). Start out with lighter weights and increase gradually.

Kb= kettlebell
KBS= kettlebell swings

Beginner's workout

Every box is a different workout. Choose one and do it.
No excuses.

Please plan your warm-up for these workouts
according to the guidelines mentioned in Chapter 2.

S. No	Add a tick mark once you complete this exercise	Date completed	Workout	Time taken (mention here if the workout specified a fixed time)	Rounds (fill this if the exercise specifies AMRAP	Weights used (leave empty if the workout does not specify weights)
1.			Do one air squat and take a breath (you can breathe all you want while you squat). Do two squats and take two breaths. Repeat up to ten and then count down to one.			
2.			(20 mins cut-off) Three rounds 50-m backward run, 50-m forward run, 50-m lunges, 10 burpees			

S. No	Add a tick mark once you complete this exercise	Date completed	Workout	Time taken (mention here if the workout specified a fixed time)	Rounds (fill this if the exercise specifies AMRAP	Weights used (leave empty if the workout does not specify weights)
3.			21-15-9 of air squats and push-ups for time			
4.			Run 1 mile (1.6 km) for time			
5.			Six rounds for time 10 push-ups, 10 air squats, 10 sit-ups			
6.			5 burpees, 5x100-m sprints (each for time)			
7.			Tabata run 4 mins AMRAP 10 push-ups, 10 squats			
8.			Three rounds 1 minute bridge hold, 20 sit-ups, 1 minute hollow hold, 20 leg raises			
9.			Five rounds 3 vertical jumps, 3 squats, 3 long jumps			
10.			15 mins AMRAP 20 lunges, 15 box jumps, 10 suryanamaskars, 5 burpees			

S. No	Add a tick mark once you complete this exercise	Date completed	Workout	Time taken (mention here if the workout specified a fixed time)	Rounds (fill this if the exercise specifies AMRAP	Weights used (leave empty if the workout does not specify weights)
11.			15 mins AMRAP 100-m sprint, 50 squats, 20 push-ups, 10 burpees			
12.			10-9-8-7-6-5-4-3-2-1 sets of sit-ups with a 100-m sprint between each set			
13.			Eight rounds 30-second handstand, 10 squats			
14.			Twenty rounds 5 push-ups, 5 squats, 5 sit-ups			
15.			Five rounds 200-m run, 20 lunges, 10 suryanamaskars, 25-m bear crawls			
16.			Three rounds 10 handstand push-ups for 30 seconds each, 200-m run			
17.			Tabata (20 seconds on, 10 seconds off, eight rounds) Alternate between squats and push-ups			

S. No	Add a tick mark once you complete this exercise	Date completed	Workout	Time taken (mention here if the workout specified a fixed time)	Rounds (fill this if the exercise specifies AMRAP	Weights used (leave empty if the workout does not specify weights)
18.			Ten rounds 10 push-ups, 10 sit-ups, 10 squats			
19.			Three rounds 800-m run, 50 air squats			
20.			100 air squats for time			
21.			Three rounds 200-m run, 10 squats, 10 push-ups			
22.			Three rounds 200-m sprint, 25 push-ups			
23.			Ten rounds 10 push-ups, 100-m dash			
24.			Tabata squats			
25.			5x400-m sprints			
26.			10x100-m dash			
27.			25 pressing snatch balances for each arm. No weights			
28.			Run 1 km, lunging 30 steps every 1 minute			
29.			Four rounds for time 10 vertical jumps, 10 push-ups, 10 sit-ups			

S. No	Add a tick mark once you complete this exercise	Date completed	Workout	Time taken (mention here if the workout specified a fixed time)	Rounds (fill this if the exercise specifies AMRAP	Weights used (leave empty if the workout does not specify weights)
30.			100 push-ups for time			
31.			Three rounds 50 sit-ups, 400-m run/ sprint/walk			
32.			Five rounds 10 vertical jumps, 400-m run			
33.			50 split jumps for time			
34.			Ten rounds 10 walking lunges, 10 push-ups			
35.			Four rounds 400-m run, 50 air squats			
36.			Ten rounds 100-m sprint, 100-m walk			
37.			Five rounds 10 vertical jumps (jump as high as you can, land, and do it again), 10 push-ups			
38.			Five rounds Burpee to the push-up position, do 10 push-ups, and then complete the burpee			

S. No	Add a tick mark once you complete this exercise	Date completed	Workout	Time taken (mention here if the workout specified a fixed time)	Rounds (fill this if the exercise specifies AMRAP	Weights used (leave empty if the workout does not specify weights)
39.			Ten rounds for time 10 burpees, 100-m sprint			
40.			Three rounds 800-m run, 60 squats			
41.			Ten rounds Plebs plank, bottom of squat, hollow rock hold for 30 seconds each (Use the transition time as rest periods. They should be as brief as possible.)			
42.			250 jumping jacks for time			
43.			Eight rounds 100-m sprint, 30 squats			
44.			Three rounds 30 push-ups, 30-second handstand or Plebs plank			
45.			Run 1 km with 100 air squats at midpoint for time			
46.			100 burpees for time			

S. No	Add a tick mark once you complete this exercise	Date completed	Workout	Time taken (mention here if the workout specified a fixed time)	Rounds (fill this if the exercise specifies AMRAP	Weights used (leave empty if the workout does not specify weights)
47.			Seven rounds for time 7 squats, 7 burpees			
48.			20 mins AMRAP 20 overhead lunges with 10 kg/5 kg, 30 push-ups, 40 sit-ups			
49.			Five rounds 50 air squats Rest for the same time it took you for each round.			
50.			Ten rounds 5 push-ups, 30-second Plebs plank, 3x100-m dash @ 80% effort			
51.			Tabata push-ups			
52.			100 jumping jacks, 75 air squats, 50 push-ups, 25 burpees for time			
53.			Five rounds 800-m run, 30 sit-ups, 30 back extensions			
54.			20 mins AMRAP 30 burpees, 100-m run, 20 V-ups			

S. No	Add a tick mark once you complete this exercise	Date completed	Workout	Time taken (mention here if the workout specified a fixed time)	Rounds (fill this if the exercise specifies AMRAP	Weights used (leave empty if the workout does not specify weights)
55.			Ten rounds 20 push-ups, 100-m sprint, 10 burpees			
56.			Five rounds 20 incline push-ups, 300-m sprint (1 min rest after each round)			
57.			Five rounds 400-m run, 30 burpees, 30 sit-ups, 30 push-ups, 30 squat jumps			
58.			Seven rounds 400-m run, 200-m run backwards 21 KBS with 12 kg/8 kg, 12 burpees			
59.			Five rounds 400-m run, 30 KBS with 16 kg, 30 sandbags clean-n-press, 30-second handstand hold			
60.			100 hollow rocks, 10 V-ups for every time you stop			

Full-length workouts

Most of these include a warm-up, main workout and a lighter cool-down section. Progress to these only after you have mastered the beginner's workout.

S. No	Add a tick mark once you complete this exercise	Date completed	Workout	Time taken (mention here if the workout specified a fixed time)	Rounds (fill this if the exercise specifies AMRAP)	Weights used (leave empty if the workout does not specify weights)
1.			**Warm-up:** 800-m run Three rounds 10 push-ups 10 squats 10 burpees **WOD (Workout of the Day):** 20 mins AMRAP, 400-m run, Maximum push-ups possible, 25 squats **After WOD:** Four rounds 1-min bridge hold, 100-m sprint			

S. No	Add a tick mark once you complete this exercise	Date completed	Workout	Time taken (mention here if the workout specified a fixed time)	Rounds (fill this if the exercise specifies AMRAP)	Weights used (leave empty if the workout does not specify weights)
2.			**Warm-up:** 400-m run, 100-m lunges, 20 push-ups, 30 squats **WOD:** 150 push-ups, 400-m penalty run for every time you stop **After WOD:** <u>Three rounds</u> Max bridge hold, 100-m sprint, 30 burpees			
3.			**Warm-up:** 400-m run, 1-min squats, 1-min push-ups, 1-min high knees **WOD:** <u>Run</u> 1600 m-800 m -400 m <u>Burpees</u> 60-30-15 <u>Lunges</u> 200 m-100 m -50 m			

S. No	Add a tick mark once you complete this exercise	Date completed	Workout	Time taken (mention here if the workout specified a fixed time)	Rounds (fill this if the exercise specifies AMRAP)	Weights used (leave empty if the workout does not specify weights)
4.			**Warm up:** 500-m run Three rounds 10 push-ups, 10 suryanamaskars, 20 shoulder dislocates **Mobility WOD:** Shoulder rotators **WOD:** 20 mins AMRAP 5 push press with 30 kg/20 kg (from standing position), 10 strict pull-ups, 5 db/Kb power clean with 10 kg/5 kg, 10 burpees **After WOD:** 10 mins AMRAP Thrusters with 20 kg/15 kg			

S. No	Add a tick mark once you complete this exercise	Date completed	Workout	Time taken (mention here if the workout specified a fixed time)	Rounds (fill this if the exercise specifies AMRAP)	Weights used (leave empty if the workout does not specify weights)
5.			**Warm-up:** 500-m run <u>Three rounds</u> 50 high knees, 20 lunges, 10 squats **Mobility WOD:** Hips **WOD:** EMONTM for 20 mins 2 back squats with 40 kg/30 kg, 4 chest-to-bar pull-ups **After WOD:** 50 squats with 25 kg/15 kg (For each time you rest the bar on the stand, do 25 burpees)			

S. No	Add a tick mark once you complete this exercise	Date completed	Workout	Time taken (mention here if the workout specified a fixed time)	Rounds (fill this if the exercise specifies AMRAP)	Weights used (leave empty if the workout does not specify weights)
6.			**Warm-up:** 500-m run, 20 lunges **Mobility WOD:** Upper and lower back **WOD:** 20 mins to reach your 3-rep max and 1 rep max for dead lifts **After WOD:** 21-15-9 Cleans with 30 kg/20 kg, Box jumps 18/12 inches high			

S. No	Add a tick mark once you complete this exercise	Date completed	Workout	Time taken (mention here if the workout specified a fixed time)	Rounds (fill this if the exercise specifies AMRAP)	Weights used (leave empty if the workout does not specify weights)
7.			**Warm-up:** 500-m run Three rounds (30 seconds each) Squats, Push-ups, Sit-ups, Burpees **Mobility WOD:** Hips Shoulders Back **WOD:** 20 mins cut-off (Reach for your 7 rep max dead lift) **After WOD:** 20 mins cut-off, 45 back squats with 35 kg/25 kg, 45 chest-to-bar pull-ups, 45 box jumps 18/12 inches high, 45 HSPU			

S. No	Add a tick mark once you complete this exercise	Date completed	Workout	Time taken (mention here if the workout specified a fixed time)	Rounds (fill this if the exercise specifies AMRAP)	Weights used (leave empty if the workout does not specify weights)
8.			**Warm-up:** 500-m run Three rounds 10 suryanamaskars, 10 KBS with 12 kg/8 kg **Mobility WOD:** Shoulders **WOD:** For time: Four rounds 12 pull-ups, 12 burpees, 4 cleans with 30 kg/25 kg 12 burpees			

S. No	Add a tick mark once you complete this exercise	Date completed	Workout	Time taken (mention here if the workout specified a fixed time)	Rounds (fill this if the exercise specifies AMRAP)	Weights used (leave empty if the workout does not specify weights)
9.			**Warm-up:** 1-km run Three rounds 5 pull-ups, 10 push-ups, 15 squats **Core:** 7 mins AMRAP 10 Supermans (knees 2 elbows each leg), 10 V-sit-ups, 50 hollow rocks **WOD:** 45 power cleans with 30 kg/20 kg, 45 box jumps 18/12 inches, 45 strict pull-ups, 45 HSPU/ 75 push-ups Scale as need be. Go through with the full range of motion **After WOD:** 1.6-km run		/	

S. No	Add a tick mark once you complete this exercise	Date completed	Workout	Time taken (mention here if the workout specified a fixed time)	Rounds (fill this if the exercise specifies AMRAP)	Weights used (leave empty if the workout does not specify weights)
10.			**Warm-up:** 500-m run Three rounds 20 lunges, 15 squats, 10 burpees **Skill:** Pistols **WOD:** 5-5-5 Back squats 3-3 Front squats **After WOD:** Four rounds 45 secs on 15 secs off Squat cleans with 30 kg/20 kg, Toes-to-bar Kbps with 12 kg/8 kg			

S. No	Add a tick mark once you complete this exercise	Date completed	Workout	Time taken (mention here if the workout specified a fixed time)	Rounds (fill this if the exercise specifies AMRAP)	Weights used (leave empty if the workout does not specify weights)
11.			**Warm-up:** 2 mins each Running, Skipping, Lunges, Burpees, Suryanamaskars **Mobility WOD:** Hips Back **WOD:** 5-5-5 Dead lifts (standing on platform) Remember these dead lifts are not for max loads but for conditioning the first pull off the ground 5-3-3-1-1 Dead lifts **After WOD:** 20 mins AMRAP 6 back squats with 40 kg/30 kg, 12 db clean with 10 kg/5 kg, 24 knees-to-elbows			

S. No	Add a tick mark once you complete this exercise	Date completed	Workout	Time taken (mention here if the workout specified a fixed time)	Rounds (fill this if the exercise specifies AMRAP)	Weights used (leave empty if the workout does not specify weights)
12.			**Warm-up:** 500-m run Three rounds 50 high knees, 30 lunges, 20 jumping squats **Mobility WOD:** Hips Back **WOD:** 3-3-3-3-3 Back squats **After WOD:** Three rounds for time 15 mins cut-off, 10 overhead squats (OHS) with 20 kg/10 kg, 15 KBS with 12 kg/8 kg, 20 pull-ups			

S. No	Add a tick mark once you complete this exercise	Date completed	Workout	Time taken (mention here if the workout specified a fixed time)	Rounds (fill this if the exercise specifies AMRAP)	Weights used (leave empty if the workout does not specify weights)
13.			**Warm-up:** 500-m run <u>Three rounds</u> 10 KBS @ 12 kg/8 kg alternate hands, 10 suryanamaskars **WOD:** 10 rounds, 10 L-sit pull-ups/ strict pull-ups, 10 deficient HSPU/push-ups (hands off the floor) **After WOD:** 700-m run			

S. No	Add a tick mark once you complete this exercise	Date completed	Workout	Time taken (mention here if the workout specified a fixed time)	Rounds (fill this if the exercise specifies AMRAP)	Weights used (leave empty if the workout does not specify weights)
14.			**Warm-up:** 500-m run Three rounds 30 tuck jumps, 20 squat jumps, 10 suryanamaskars **Core:** Two rounds 1 min knees-to-elbow, 1 min L-sit hold, 1 min hollow rock **WOD:** 40 min cut-off for time 150 wall-ball shots with 6 kg/3 kg, 50 burpee box jumps 18/12 inches high 25 power cleans with 30 kg/20 kg **After WOD:** 2-km run			

S. No	Add a tick mark once you complete this exercise	Date completed	Workout	Time taken (mention here if the workout specified a fixed time)	Rounds (fill this if the exercise specifies AMRAP)	Weights used (leave empty if the workout does not specify weights)
15.			**Warm-up:** 500-m run, 7 suryanamaskars **Mobility WOD:** Shoulder Hips Back **WOD:** For time: 400-m row, 25 HSPU, 50 back squats with 30 kg/20 kg, 100 pull-ups **After WOD:** 7 mins AMRAP Max bridge holds, Max hollow rocks			

S. No	Add a tick mark once you complete this exercise	Date completed	Workout	Time taken (mention here if the workout specified a fixed time)	Rounds (fill this if the exercise specifies AMRAP)	Weights used (leave empty if the workout does not specify weights)
16.			**Warm-up:** Three rounds 20 OHS, 20 lunges, 50 skips **Mobility WOD:** Hips **WOD:** Back squats 5-5-3-3-1 1x15 at desired weight **After WOD:** Three rounds: (for time) 15 mins cut-off 5 dead lifts with 50 kg/30 kg, 10 HSPU/ push-ups, 20 burpees			

S. No	Add a tick mark once you complete this exercise	Date completed	Workout	Time taken (mention here if the workout specified a fixed time)	Rounds (fill this if the exercise specifies AMRAP)	Weights used (leave empty if the workout does not specify weights)
17.			**Warm-up:** Stretch Three rounds 10 push-ups 10 KBS **SKILL:** Bench press **WOD:** 20 mins cut-off Five rounds for maximum reps Bench press with body weight, Pull-ups (Rest as you wish) **After WOD:** 500-m run, 50 toes to-bar, 50 hollow rocks, Max bridge hold			

S. No	Add a tick mark once you complete this exercise	Date completed	Workout	Time taken (mention here if the workout specified a fixed time)	Rounds (fill this if the exercise specifies AMRAP)	Weights used (leave empty if the workout does not specify weights)
18.			**Warm up:** 500-m run Three rounds 20 sit-ups, 20 back extensions, 1 min bridge hold **Mobility WOD:** Shoulders Back **WOD:** 20 mins cut-off, Reach your 5 rep, 3 rep, and 1 rep max for dead lifts **After WOD:** 12 mins cut-off Three rounds 30 db snatch with 10 kg/5 kg (Alternate hands), 20 hands-off push-ups, 10 pull-ups			

S. No	Add a tick mark once you complete this exercise	Date completed	Workout	Time taken (mention here if the workout specified a fixed time)	Rounds (fill this if the exercise specifies AMRAP)	Weights used (leave empty if the workout does not specify weights)
19.			**Warm-up:** 750-m run **Mobility WOD:** Shoulders Back **WOD:** (For time) 30 thrusters with 25 kg/15 kg, 50 strict pull-ups, 30 dead lifts with 50 kg/35 kg, 50 push-ups 30 KBS with 12 kg/8 kg, 50 knees-to-elbows, 30 db snatches with 10 kg/5 kg (15 each hand), 50 double unders			

S. No	Add a tick mark once you complete this exercise	Date completed	Workout	Time taken (mention here if the workout specified a fixed time)	Rounds (fill this if the exercise specifies AMRAP)	Weights used (leave empty if the workout does not specify weights)
20.			**Warm-up:** 500-m run Three rounds 3 wall climbs, 7 burpees, 10 med ball cleans **Mobility WOD:** Wrist flexibility Elbows Shoulder Neck **WOD:** (20 mins) 'Kettlebell skill work' Learning Rack position, Clean from dead hang position, Clean from swing, Strict press Push press **After WOD:** (Choose a weight that is not too heavy, you should be able to do the first round in one go)			

S. No	Add a tick mark once you complete this exercise	Date completed	Workout	Time taken (mention here if the workout specified a fixed time)	Rounds (fill this if the exercise specifies AMRAP)	Weights used (leave empty if the workout does not specify weights)
			15 mins AMRAP 15 KBS all the way to the top, 10 R-arm clean and push press, 15 KBS, 10 L-arm clean and push press, 15 pull-ups			
21.			**Warm-up:** 500-m run Three rounds (30 seconds each) Push-ups, High knees, Burpees, Squats **Mobility WOD:** Shoulder Hips **WOD:** Skill work, Double arm Kb clean and press Three rounds 10 double arm Kb clean and press, 10 burpees			

S. No	Add a tick mark once you complete this exercise	Date completed	Workout	Time taken (mention here if the workout specified a fixed time)	Rounds (fill this if the exercise specifies AMRAP)	Weights used (leave empty if the workout does not specify weights)
			After WOD: 12 mins AMRAP Thrusters with 25 kg/15 kg, Pull-ups, Increase the reps by one each time. So, 1,1 2,2 3,3 Keep going till time runs out			
22.			Warm-up: 800-m run Mobility WOD: Stretch (suryanamaskars) WOD: For time (45mins cut-off) 100 thrusters with 20 kg/15 kg, 100 pull-ups, 100 KBS with 12 kg/8 kg, 100 pistols (alternating legs)			

S. No	Add a tick mark once you complete this exercise	Date completed	Workout	Time taken (mention here if the workout specified a fixed time)	Rounds (fill this if the exercise specifies AMRAP)	Weights used (leave empty if the workout does not specify weights)
23.			**Warm-up:** Three rounds (30 seconds each) High knees, Burpees, Butt kicks, Suryanamaskars **Mobility WOD:** Back Shoulders **WOD:** Five rounds (1 min each) L-sit hold, Handstand hold, Hollow rock, Bridge hold **After WOD:** 500-m run			

S. No	Add a tick mark once you complete this exercise	Date completed	Workout	Time taken (mention here if the workout specified a fixed time)	Rounds (fill this if the exercise specifies AMRAP)	Weights used (leave empty if the workout does not specify weights)
24.			**Warm-up:** 500-m run, 40 push-ups 20 suryanamaskars **Mobility WOD:** Shoulders **WOD:** 20 mins cut-off 5 reps bench press **After WOD:** 21-15-9 Thrusters with 30 kg/20 kg, Pull-ups			

S. No	Add a tick mark once you complete this exercise	Date completed	Workout	Time taken (mention here if the workout specified a fixed time)	Rounds (fill this if the exercise specifies AMRAP)	Weights used (leave empty if the workout does not specify weights)
25.			**Warm-up:** 500-m run <u>Three rounds</u> 7 suryanamaskars, 10 OHS, 15 V-ups **Mobility WOD:** Shoulder Hips Lower back **WOD:** 20 mins AMRAP 5 strict pull-ups, 10 push-ups, 15 squats Now this is how you should do this workout. In cycles of five rounds, the pull-ups remain strict throughout <u>Push-ups:</u> Body weight-10 kg-15 kg-20 kg-25 kg, and then repeat <u>Squats:</u> Body weight-10 kg-15 kg-20 kg-25 kg **After WOD:** 50 strict toes-to-bar/V sit-ups			

S. No	Add a tick mark once you complete this exercise	Date completed	Workout	Time taken (mention here if the workout specified a fixed time)	Rounds (fill this if the exercise specifies AMRAP)	Weights used (leave empty if the workout does not specify weights)
26.			**Warm-up:** 500-m run Three rounds 10 wall-ball shots, 10 push-ups **Mobility WOD:** 1 min shoulder mobility, 1 min mobility, 1 min back mobility **WOD:** E2MONTM (Every Two Minutes on the minute) For 10 mins 3 push presses with increasing weights **After WOD:** 12 mins AMRAP 10 db thrusters with 7.5 kg/5 kg, 10 toes-to-bar, 10 KBS with 12 kg/8 kg			

S. No	Add a tick mark once you complete this exercise	Date completed	Workout	Time taken (mention here if the workout specified a fixed time)	Rounds (fill this if the exercise specifies AMRAP)	Weights used (leave empty if the workout does not specify weights)
27.			**Warm-up:** 500-m run, 30 medicine ball cleans **Mobility WOD:** 1 min shoulder extension rotation (lying down), 1 min tricep stretch, 1 min latt mobility, 1 min shoulder mobility **WOD:** E2M for 10 mins, 2 hang power cleans with increasing weight (Work towards your best) **After WOD:** <u>Three rounds for time</u> 10 power cleans with 30 kg/20 kg, 20 pull-ups, 30 burpees			

S. No	Add a tick mark once you complete this exercise	Date completed	Workout	Time taken (mention here if the workout specified a fixed time)	Rounds (fill this if the exercise specifies AMRAP)	Weights used (leave empty if the workout does not specify weights)
28.			**Warm-up:** 500-m run, 30 push-ups, 30 Kb Sumo Dead lift High Pull (sdhp) with 12 kg/8 kg, 30 jumping squats			
			Mobility WOD: 1 min shoulder dislocates, 1 min downward dog, roll into upward dog, 1 min band stretch (each arm)			
			WOD: <u>Five rounds</u> for time (complete in any order) 400-m run, 10 strict press with 25 kg/20 kg (No push press or jerk allowed), 15 strict pull-ups			
			After WOD: 100 hollow rocks			

S. No	Add a tick mark once you complete this exercise	Date completed	Workout	Time taken (mention here if the workout specified a fixed time)	Rounds (fill this if the exercise specifies AMRAP)	Weights used (leave empty if the workout does not specify weights)
29.			**Warm-up:** 500-m run Three rounds 3 wall climbs, 6 suryanamaskars, 9 KBS **Mobility WOD:** 1 min hollow hold, 1 min Superman, 1 min side-split hold (each side), 1 min front split, 1 min back mobility **WOD:** Five rounds 30 supine runs, 30 push-ups, 30 toes-to-bar, 30 pistols (15 for each leg), 500-m run **After WOD:** 15 head-to-ground HSPU			

S. No	Add a tick mark once you complete this exercise	Date completed	Workout	Time taken (mention here if the workout specified a fixed time)	Rounds (fill this if the exercise specifies AMRAP)	Weights used (leave empty if the workout does not specify weights)
30.			**Warm-up:** 500-m run			
			<u>Three rounds</u> (30 seconds each) Push-ups, Squats, Jumping pull-ups, Bridge hold			
			Mobility WOD: Triceps roll-out (1 min each arm), Shoulder twist (30 seconds each arm), Triceps stretch (30 seconds each arm)			
			WOD: 12 mins AMRAP 5 muscle snatch from hang position with 25 kg/15 kg, 7 HSPU/14 hands off the floor push-ups			
			After WOD: 10 mins AMRAP 15 squats, 7 burpees			

S. No	Add a tick mark once you complete this exercise	Date completed	Workout	Time taken (mention here if the workout specified a fixed time)	Rounds (fill this if the exercise specifies AMRAP)	Weights used (leave empty if the workout does not specify weights)
31.			**Warm-up:** 500-m run, Stretch, Squat, Push-up mobilizes **Mobility WOD:** Elbows, triceps, shoulders **WOD:** Power/hang lean and press with 30 kg/20 kg 2-4-6 Burpees 21-15-9 (If you want to challenge yourself, go heavier than the recommended weight) Rest for 2 mins once you finish, after which complete a 7 mins AMRAP 7 HSPU, 7 KBS with 12 kg/8 kg			

S. No	Add a tick mark once you complete this exercise	Date completed	Workout	Time taken (mention here if the workout specified a fixed time)	Rounds (fill this if the exercise specifies AMRAP)	Weights used (leave empty if the workout does not specify weights)
32.			**Warm-up:** 500-m run Mobilize **Mobility WOD:** Overall **WOD:** No cut-off for time 60 strict pull-ups, 60 HSPU/hands off the floor push-ups, 60 toes-to-bar, 60 pistols, 500-m run **After WOD:** 7-min bridge hold			

S. No	Add a tick mark once you complete this exercise	Date completed	Workout	Time taken (mention here if the workout specified a fixed time)	Rounds (fill this if the exercise specifies AMRAP)	Weights used (leave empty if the workout does not specify weights)
33.			**Warm up:** 500-m run Three rounds 10 suryanamaskars, 20 squats **Mobility WOD:** Hips and lower back **WOD:** 30 mins cut-off Five rounds 12 dead lifts with 40 kg/30 kg, 9 hang power cleans, 6 front squats (1 min rest after each round) **After WOD:** 500-m run, 50 weighted sit-ups with 8 kg/6 kg			

S. No	Add a tick mark once you complete this exercise	Date completed	Workout	Time taken (mention here if the workout specified a fixed time)	Rounds (fill this if the exercise specifies AMRAP)	Weights used (leave empty if the workout does not specify weights)
34.			**Warm-up:** 800-m run Three rounds 15 squats, 10 suryanamaskars **Mobility WOD:** Hips Shoulders **WOD:** 20 mins or goal achieved, whichever comes first 100 thrusters with 20 kg/15 kg Do 5 burpees for every extra minute **After WOD:** 100 hollow rocks			

S. No	Add a tick mark once you complete this exercise	Date completed	Workout	Time taken (mention here if the workout specified a fixed time)	Rounds (fill this if the exercise specifies AMRAP)	Weights used (leave empty if the workout does not specify weights)
35.			**Warm Up:** 500-m run Three rounds 15 wall-ball shots, 7 suryanamaskars **Mobility WOD:** Back Hamstrings **WOD:** Seven rounds 7 dead lifts with 50 kg/30 kg, 14 push-ups **After WOD:** Four rounds 400-m run, 21 knees-to-elbows			

S. No	Add a tick mark once you complete this exercise	Date completed	Workout	Time taken (mention here if the workout specified a fixed time)	Rounds (fill this if the exercise specifies AMRAP)	Weights used (leave empty if the workout does not specify weights)
36.			**Warm-up:** 500-m run Three rounds 10 shoulder dislocates, 10 suryanamaskars, 10 wall-ball shots **Mobility WOD:** Shoulder Rotator cuffs Chest **WOD:** 20 mins AMRAP for total reps 3 power cleans with 30 kg/20 kg, 4 push press with 30 kg/20 kg, 5 burpees, 6 strict pull-ups **After WOD:** 10 mins AMRAP 1-min L-sit hold, 15 toes-to-bar, 25 hollow rocks			

S. No	Add a tick mark once you complete this exercise	Date completed	Workout	Time taken (mention here if the workout specified a fixed time)	Rounds (fill this if the exercise specifies AMRAP)	Weights used (leave empty if the workout does not specify weights)
37.			**Warm-up:** 500-m run Three rounds 10 OHS, 10 medicine ball cleans, 10 suryanamaskars **Mobility WOD:** Shoulders Back **WOD:** 20 mins time cap 'snatch' **After WOD:** 15 mins AMRAP 7 OHS with 20 kg/10 kg, 10 pull-ups, 14 burpees			

S. No	Add a tick mark once you complete this exercise	Date completed	Workout	Time taken (mention here if the workout specified a fixed time)	Rounds (fill this if the exercise specifies AMRAP)	Weights used (leave empty if the workout does not specify weights)
38.			**Warm-up:** 500-m run 21-15-9 Squats Push-ups Medicine ball cleans **Mobility WOD:** Shoulders Rotator cuff **WOD:** 20 mins AMRAP Ladder Climb (increments of 3), Overhead press with 30 kg/20 kg, strict pull-ups KBS with 12 kg/8 kg **After WOD:** 10 mins (Change exercise after you can't do any more reps) L-sit hold, Bridge			

S. No	Add a tick mark once you complete this exercise	Date completed	Workout	Time taken (mention here if the workout specified a fixed time)	Rounds (fill this if the exercise specifies AMRAP)	Weights used (leave empty if the workout does not specify weights)
39.			**Warm-up:** 500-m run Three rounds 10 medicine ball cleans, 10 push-ups, 10 burpees **MobilityWOD:** Shoulders **WOD:** 20 mins AMRAP 500-m run, 30 flat bench press with 30 kg/20 kg, 50 KBS with 12 kg/8 kg **After WOD:** Tabata Squats, Pull-ups			

S. No	Add a tick mark once you complete this exercise	Date completed	Workout	Time taken (mention here if the workout specified a fixed time)	Rounds (fill this if the exercise specifies AMRAP)	Weights used (leave empty if the workout does not specify weights)
40.			**Warm-up:** 500-m run, Work on mobility **WOD:** Every two mins for 20 mins, 3 power snatches (Increase weights with each round if you wish. NO CLEAN AND PRESS should be mistaken for a SNATCH.) **After WOD:** 10 mins AMRAP 10 db/Kb snatch with 10 kg/5 kg (5 for each hand), 10 knees-to- elbows/sit-ups, 5 burpees			

S. No	Add a tick mark once you complete this exercise	Date completed	Workout	Time taken (mention here if the workout specified a fixed time)	Rounds (fill this if the exercise specifies AMRAP)	Weights used (leave empty if the workout does not specify weights)
41.			Warm-up: 500-m run Three rounds 20 squats 5 burpees WOD: 'Bring Sally up, bring Sally down' Play the song and every time you hear the word 'down', go down, and every time it says 'up', stand up			

S. No	Add a tick mark once you complete this exercise	Date completed	Workout	Time taken (mention here if the workout specified a fixed time)	Rounds (fill this if the exercise specifies AMRAP)	Weights used (leave empty if the workout does not specify weights)
42.			**Warm-up:** 500-m run Three rounds 3 wall climbs, 7 suryanamaskars, 10 shoulder dislocates, both front and back **Mobility WOD:** Shoulders Neck Triceps **WOD:** 3 shoulder press (Every 2 mins for 20 mins). Start at a comfortable weight and increase gradually. Once you are close to the maximum, increase in small amounts **After WOD:** 10 mins AMRAP 10 db/Kb clean and press with 10 kg/5 kg, 10 push-ups, 10 burpees			

S. No	Add a tick mark once you complete this exercise	Date completed	Workout	Time taken (mention here if the workout specified a fixed time)	Rounds (fill this if the exercise specifies AMRAP)	Weights used (leave empty if the workout does not specify weights)
43.			**Warm-up:** 500-m run, 50 squats, 30 lunges **Mobility WOD:** Hips Back **WOD:** (Every two mins for 20 mins) 5 back squats with increasing weights (Start with a comfortable weight and then increase after every two rounds. Once you are close to your limit, increase by small weights) **After WOD:** 10 mins AMRAP 7 overhead squats with 25 kg/15 kg, 14 weighted lunges with 15 kg/10 kg (7 for each leg), 7 burpees			

S. No	Add a tick mark once you complete this exercise	Date completed	Workout	Time taken (mention here if the workout specified a fixed time)	Rounds (fill this if the exercise specifies AMRAP)	Weights used (leave empty if the workout does not specify weights)
44.			**Warm-up:** 500-m run, <u>Three rounds</u> 15 med ball cleans, 15 push-ups **Mobility WOD:** Hips Ankles **WOD:** 21-15-9 Squat cleans with 30 kg/20 kg, Handstand push-ups/hands off the floor push-ups **After WOD:** <u>Three rounds</u> Max L-sit hold, 10 L-sit pull-ups, 15 hollow rocks			

S. No	Add a tick mark once you complete this exercise	Date completed	Workout	Time taken (mention here if the workout specified a fixed time)	Rounds (fill this if the exercise specifies AMRAP)	Weights used (leave empty if the workout does not specify weights)
45.			**Warm-up:** 500-m run Three rounds 3 wall climbs, 10 push ups, 15 medicine ball cleans **Mobility WOD:** Shoulder Back **WOD:** 20 mins cut-off 3-3-3-3-3 Push jerk **After WOD:** 12 mins AMRAP 40 HSPU/push-ups hands-off/30 wall climbs, 60 pull-ups 80 KBS with 12 kg/8 kg			

Acknowledgements

I would like to say a big thank you to:

My parents, Ashok and Reeta Bhatt, for bringing me into the world and allowing me to become who I am today,

To my brother, Kirnay Bhatt, for being the first one to join me in my CrossFit journey,

To my late swimming coach, Mr Subodh Danke, for pushing me throughout my swimming career,

And last, but not the least, my spiritual partner and better half, Vrinda, without whom 'Shivoham' and Shivfit would not have happened.

A Note on the Authors

Shivoham

A former professional swimmer and water polo player, Shivoham has trained Bollywood actors Aamir Khan, Abhishek Bachchan, Sonakshi Sinha, Jacqueline Fernandez, Neha Dhupia, Ranveer Singh, Jacky Bhagnani, Arjun Kapoor, Shraddha Kapoor, Anil Kapoor, John Abraham, Parineeti Chopra, Shaad Ali and Ayan Mukherjee, who swear by his diet and workout regime.

Shivoham combines gymnastics, weightlifting and strength conditioning to ensure all his clients at CrossFitOM, his gym in Mumbai, are fit. He also guides them as a nutritionist and physiotherapist.

He ascribes to the philosophy that the fitness journey starts in the mind and training it is just as important as physical exercise in order to achieve fitness goals.

Shrenik Avlani

Shrenik is a newsroom veteran with nearly two decades of work experience with leading newspapers including the *Hindustan Times* and *Deccan Chronicle*, and sports bodies such as the BCCI.

On a break from full-time work since 2012, he has also covered the FIFA Football World Cup and the Olympics. As a leading writer in the field of endurance sport and fitness, he contributes to the *Mint*, *Vogue*, *The Hindu*, *GQ*, *National Geographic Traveller*, *FirstPost*, *Mumbai Mirror*, *Bangalore Mirror*, *Sports Illustrated*, *Guardian* and other publications in Dubai and England.

Shrenik uses his new-found freedom to explore the world, keep fit and catch up on sleep. He has lectured at Symbiosis Commerce College (Pune), Christ University (Bangalore) and Wichita State University (Kansas, USA).